PROPA-
GANDA
DECODED

Political shock waves are currently rattling Western democracies. From hatred and anger to fake news and alleged conspiracies, polarization is one of the central social issues of our time. In recent years, we have seen the emergence of politicians and political parties that dominate democratic debates with implacable and heated rhetoric. This is a deliberate propaganda strategy. It is designed to disrupt all dialogue in our society and politics—and thus to strike at the very core of our democracies. To fight this many-headed monster, we must see through the propaganda; only by doing so can we develop counterstrategies and protect our democracies.

PROPAGANDA DECODED

How Manipulation Endangers Democracy

By Birand Bingül

Translated by Oliver Latsch

W1-Media, Inc.
Grand Books
Stamford, CT, USA

Copyright © 2023 by W1-Media Inc. for this edition
Original title: Alles Propaganda!
Wie Manipulation unsere Demokratie gefährdet
© 2023 by Atrium AG, Zurich
First English edition published by
W1-Media Inc./Grand Books 2023

Visit our website at www.arctis-books.com

1 3 5 7 9 8 6 4 2

The Library of Congress Control Number: 2023932899
ISBN 978-1-64690-031-2
eBook ISBN 978-1-64690-637-6
English translation copyright © Oliver Latsch, 2023

Printed in China

Introduction
Monsters and Shock Waves

If you're reading this book, there's a good chance you follow the news or use social media on a regular basis. In that case, it probably hasn't escaped your notice that for some years now the Western world has been rocked by political shock waves, which have particularly been rolling through the liberal democracies of Europe and the United States. Time and time again, there is fresh anger, hatred, fake news, and alleged conspiracies. Attacks on parliaments and parliamentarians, courts and judges, academic institutions and researchers, and media outlets and journalists have been reported. It has not stopped there. In recent years, there have been politically motivated murders in many countries. Polarization is one of the central social phenomena of our time. Right-wing populists and authoritarians are generally identified as being responsible for this. In practically all Western countries, politicians and parties in recent years have established themselves in ways that can be called anything from populist to authoritarian: Donald Trump in the United States, Putin in Russia, Erdoğan in Turkey, Orbán in Hungary, and the AfD (Alternative fur Deutschland) in Germany. In Europe, right-wingers can also be found in Belgium, Denmark, England, Finland, France, Greece, Italy, the Netherlands, Austria, Poland, Sweden, Switzerland, Slovakia, Spain, and the Czech Republic. But there are also left-wing variants, such as Syriza in Greece and Podemos in Spain. The list is long. And there is no end to their electoral successes. In the fall of 2022, Giorgia Meloni won the election with the radical right-wing Fratelli d'Italia and became prime minister of Italy. Shortly before that, the Sweden right-winger Democrats won more than 20 percent of the vote and became an influential force in this traditionally social-democratic country.

This phenomenon of populism and authoritarianism has recently been analyzed extensively by experts from various disciplines.[1] Nevertheless, as the editor in chief of the German weekly *Die Zeit*, Giovanni di Lorenzo, stated soberly in a front-page story: "Democratic parties have yet to find effective means to counter their enemies."[2] Finnish investigative journalist Jessikka Aro concludes that Western states are "inadequate for meeting the challenges of organized online hate dissemination."[3] Aro knows what she's talking about. She has built an international reputation as an expert on Russian information warfare in the face of severe personal harassment and smear campaigns against her.

But how is it that the so-called authoritarian parties have been able to gain so much power and influence? We wonder because we do not understand well enough what these enemies do nor how and why—and without a thorough diagnosis, there can be no helpful remedy.

This book aims to contribute to such a diagnosis,

a better understanding from the perspective of a communications expert. To this end, the parties and movements labeled as populist and authoritarian must first be understood for what they are: They are parties that systematically use propaganda. They are propaganda parties. They use a complex and elaborate playbook. There is a blueprint for propaganda parties and those who aspire to be propaganda parties: strategies and actions, and terminology and techniques that come together to form a system of propaganda machinery in which the whole is greater than the sum of its parts. This propaganda concept is based, to a surprising degree, on the deeper propaganda logic of Adolf Hitler and Joseph Goebbels. Goebbels described propaganda as the "avant-garde" and the "pioneer of Realpolitik."[4] Anyone who wants to decode the present situation must come to terms with the National Socialist "fathers" of all modern propaganda. Therefore, these historical references will be repeatedly made in *Propaganda Decoded*.

Propaganda pursues specific goals. Propaganda parties seek power for power's sake. They polarize to contaminate social dialogue. If dialogue is made impossible, we experience a petrifaction of opinion forming, and democracy is paralyzed. Democracy struggles to deliver results, especially on contentious issues. All this plays further into the hands of the propaganda parties.

Propaganda deceives and seduces. It undermines and confuses. It destroys and annihilates. Anyone who wants to protect Western democracy must recognize and see through contemporary propaganda in its entirety and depth. Otherwise, counterstrategies will remain piecemeal at best, and the propagandists' advance will continue. Propaganda is the most significant contemporary monster. It has many arms and heads. And yet, standing in the middle of the political stage, it sometimes seems overlooked or invisible—with fatal consequences for liberal democracies.

Chapter 1
Propaganda Parties

To fully understand the monster of propaganda and counter its shock waves, we must first understand the nature of propaganda parties. In this context, various terms are generally bandied about, but these miss the core of the phenomenon. The term "populism," for example, is simply misleading. It focuses on the relationship of populists to the electorate. However, the desire to be the people's voice is only an affectation. It is really about seducing the populace to secure their loyalty. The vital essence is how propaganda parties communicate with the people. In other words, a politician can act populist in principle without becoming a propagandist. Many politicians in liberal democracies act populistically—at least from time to time—and it is only right they do so as representatives of the people.

On the other hand, those who speak of authoritarians are too intent on setting up a bigoted antithesis to liberal democracy. In addition, the term "authoritarian" tends to focus on the domineering behavior of the respective politicians, further obscuring the core of the matter. Descriptions such as "protest"—or "anti-politician"—are also misleading because protest and antagonism are not the essence of these parties. It is much more accurate to describe parties like the German AfD, Trump's Republicans, the Turkish AKP, or the Hungarian Fidesz as propaganda parties. The reasons for this will become apparent in a moment. Such parties are, at their core, propagandists. Propaganda politicians lead them.

According to standard definitions, propaganda has a negative connotation. Propaganda can be characterized as very aggressive, ideologically motivated political communication carried out on a massive and permanent scale. Propaganda aims to influence with all available means, particularly dishonest and manipulative ones, toward a particular goal and in a certain way, especially when it comes to changing people's emotions, opinions, and behavior. The actual plans and interests behind such propaganda are obscured. Parties that submit to propaganda place it at the beginning and center of their political action. In such parties, all political activity serves a propagandist function. The electorate and the content are secondary. Their politics is propaganda. Propaganda is their policy.

What all propaganda parties have in common is that they invest a conspicuous amount of resources into their communications work. They have the largest communication departments and are more active on social media than other parties. They pursue creating and using their own media and other channels to reach the electorate. It is typical for propaganda parties to, on the one hand, attack established media and, on the other, appear in them wherever possible and ideally gain power over them in general.

Propaganda work is influenced not only by politicians but also by political advisers, communicators, specialized media agencies, opinion researchers, and pollsters, who often provide the internal party strategy for propagandistic core messages and actions. Troll factories or troll farms should also be mentioned here. Paid trolls deliberately spread false information on the Internet to manipulate opinions, influence election results, and silence critics. The best-known troll factory is the Internet Research Agency in Saint Petersburg, Russia, which, among other activities, has influenced elections in the United States and Europe. Although Russia's president, Putin, claims it is a privately run institution, there is some evidence that this troll factory is state controlled.[1] According to one study, thirty governments worldwide employed troll factories in 2017.[2] When propaganda parties come into power, they are supported by collaborators in state media and intelligence services, i.e., highly functional parts of the state apparatus in terms of their potential use for propaganda.

The contemporary propaganda party deliberately recruits as many supporters as possible from a group of disappointed, worried, doubting, frightened, angry individuals. The much-invoked will of the people plays, at best, a subordinate role. In an often marginalizing, ceaseless campaign, propaganda parties attempt to gain approval through skillful and radical misuse of political communication. Propaganda parties are not driven by content; the content is ultimately arbitrarily interchangeable if it does not catch on as desired. The masses are the key to the power they crave. Once the propaganda party has won the affection of the masses, the reversal kicks in: the leaders declare what the will of the people is—and the people follow. Maximizing or maintaining this power at all costs is the propaganda party's hidden fundamental impulse. That is their sole raison d'être. Let it be repeated: propaganda parties are about power for power's sake.

The fact propaganda parties are not concerned with content can be seen, for example, in a phenomenon we might call the Uncertainty Paradox: The propaganda politicians claim that they are running to do something about the insecurity and uncertainty of the masses. But on the contrary, they constantly increase uncertainty and insecurity because this brings them closer to their covert goal.

Moreover, it is anything but a coincidence that propaganda parties are politically more often located on the right than on the left of the political spectrum. After all, they usually reference a past in which the country was supposedly better off. The people had more reason to feel national pride—a fundamental conservative motif. Especially in Europe and North America, emotional connectivity is much more significant in the conservative camp than on the left. The Russian essayist Svetlana Boym speaks of "restorative nostalgia." A past—transfigured and idealized—homeland is to be restored, and the old identity is to be given new luster. As impossible as it is to restore the past, Boym says, the supporters of restorative nostalgia act with paranoid determination, renouncing critical thinking while under the spell of grand symbolism. In this way, restorative nostalgia can give birth to monsters.[3]

It is apparent how much the propaganda politicians resemble each other in their actions and behavior. The fact they exchange strategies and copy each other is documented and unsurprising. For example, Steve Bannon, former Trump adviser and head of Breitbart News, is frequently in Europe, exchanging ideas with Alice Weidel of the AfD, the Hungarian head of government Viktor Orbán, and an adviser to Marine Le Pen. He participated in exclusive meetings of the relevant circles. Bannon wanted to unite the right-wing nationalists of Europe with his Brussels-based foundation, "The Movement." It would be naive to assume that similarities in propaganda are solely the result of fleeting agreements and a lively copy-and-paste mentality.

Yet, despite the similarities and interconnections, propaganda parties must also be appraised differentially. A brief typology will help to classify propaganda parties in their various stages and developmental phases.

In her epoch-making work *The Origins of Totalitarianism* in 1951, the philosopher Hannah Arendt, after analyzing Hitler's Nazi state and Stalin's Soviet Union, distinguished between totalitarian and pre-totalitarian propaganda. According to her work, pre-totalitarian propaganda aims to win over sympathizers and party followers. In the totalitarian world, pure indoctrination prevails. It is directed at everyone and is wholly disinhibited. Totalitarian propaganda does not allow for any other point of view and makes the coexistence of ideas impossible.[4]

Arendt's distinction between pre-totalitarian and totalitarian propaganda can be translated and refined to apply to today's conditions, especially regarding parties as propagandistic actors. Totalitarian propaganda goes hand in hand with war propaganda in a nondemocratic—at best, sham democratic—regime. In this form of propaganda, preexisting contempt for others is heightened to an ideology of annihilation. As Arendt worked out, the method of totalitarian propaganda is indoctrination—if necessary, even on a global scale. Nowadays, this also includes destabilizing propaganda through hacker attacks and troll farms that steal and spread compromising material, especially around elections. Such attacks were used to discredit candidates, such as Hillary Clinton in the United States and Emmanuel Macron in France, to influence the citizens' electoral decision. Part of totalitarian propaganda is increasing communication output to absurd levels to maintain a painstakingly constructed worldview free of cracks and fractures. Yet this also exposes the significant instability of totalitarian propaganda.

In times of war, propaganda is used intensively—and is also discussed more, following the wisdom that "in war, truth is the first casualty." Russia's war of aggression on Ukraine was accompanied by shameless, often crude war propaganda that has long been effective in Russia. Vladimir Putin, the Russian president has performed and allowed the performance of totalitarian propaganda in its purest form during the Ukraine campaign. However, totalitarian war propaganda is only the tip of the iceberg. Pre-totalitarian propaganda parties are characterized by the fact they are often the only party in government—sometimes for a long time—and have achieved certain milestones. These include, among other things, that the leader is endowed with extraordinary power and that a cult has been established around this leader.

Furthermore, pre-totalitarian propaganda parties can maintain core democratic elements while weakening institutions such as parliament and the judiciary. They also control the opposition, nongovernmental organizations, and independent media. They are characterized by communicative dominance, which significantly controls and shapes public and published discourse. As a result, pre-totalitarian propaganda can potentially organize much more stable conditions than totalitarian propaganda. Today's pre-totalitarian propaganda politicians include Viktor Orbán and Recep Tayyip Erdoğan. Pre-totalitarian propaganda parties include several subtypes. The category of voted-out pre-totalitarian propaganda parties includes, for example, Donald Trump's Republicans—with the next elections already casting their shadows. Coalition propaganda parties have made it into government but cannot govern outright. These parties currently include Poland's PiS, which Jarosław Kaczyński shaped. This party has also ruled alone and in a pre-totalitarian manner in the past. As a junior partner, for example, the Austrian FPÖ governed with the conservative party of then-Chancellor Sebastian Kurz between 2017 and

2019 before the so-called "Ibiza affair" catapulted the FPÖ out of the government.

An oppositional propaganda party is characterized by having no direct political power. Still, it exerts great influence and pressure on governing parties. It shapes crucial public debates and helps to influence decisions. As a result, it makes substantial gains in votes without winning overall victories and gaining government power. Oppositional propaganda parties include Germany's AfD during the so-called refugee crisis of 2015 and the French Rassemblement National, with Marine Le Pen's two consecutive second-place finishes in presidential elections.

Last but not least, we can identify failing propaganda parties that, for various reasons, operate unsuccessfully in opposition, fail to penetrate in terms of propaganda, and assume a marginal role, which is fatal, especially in the propaganda logic of pure group acquisition. The German AfD, in its current form, fits in here.

This typology of propaganda parties is based on a dynamic, not a mechanistic understanding: progress can be followed by a reversal and vice versa. And not every propaganda party will—or must—strive to become totalitarian.

According to the typology outlined, from a historical point of view, the German Nazi party NSDAP went through almost all stages—a failing propaganda party at the beginning, an oppositional and effective party at the end of the Weimar Republic, a pre-totalitarian party for a very short time after seizing power in 1933, and finally a totalitarian party with the beginning of the war—until its downfall. The reference to the Hitler regime is not intended to lump all these parties together in content. It is merely a matter of analyzing which communication strategies are used, how, and why.

When talking about the instrument of propaganda, we must never forget that it is not always destined to be successful. On the contrary, even if one assumes that propaganda is competently managed and carried out, there was and is no guarantee of success; countless uncontrollable variables, obstacles, and unpredictable setbacks can cause disruption. These include serious events that change the course of history; wrong decisions, missteps, and coincidences; financiers who jump ship or reorient themselves; combative competitors who fight back; internal rivalries; or drastic changes in the mood of the electorate, and so on. The uncertainties are so manifold that the number of successes of propaganda parties must be considered astounding. Nevertheless, it is worth considering this as an indication of how robust, effective, consistent, and conceptually driven propaganda work must be. What this looks like is explained step-by-step on the following pages.

Chapter 2

Roots: The Political Idea of Propaganda

It is thought that propaganda begins with the invention of a new political idea. As self-evident, even banal, as this may sound, it is not so. After all, not just any idea will do. It has to be an extraordinary idea.

Parties usually represent specific social interests. That is where they have their roots. From those interests, they draw their values and their base. In Germany, the CDU represents the conservative middle class, and the FDP represents businesses and freelancers. With its convictions, a new party usually seeks to fill a gap in the party spectrum and uplift a particular interest that seems unoccupied or neglected and promising. The merger of the East German Party of Democratic Socialism (PDS) and the West German Electoral Alternative Work and Social Justice (WASG), for example, occupied the gap to the left of the Social Democrats—and so the new party logically called itself the Left (Die Linke). Classic party-political positioning.

Propaganda parties act differently right from the start. Their idea has to be propagandistically useful, and Hitler was already very aware of this. In his eyes, the new political idea had to have the potential to electrify the masses and maximize his power. Gaining power was the goal to which everything had to be subservient. A political idea that did not promote this goal was useless. Without a political idea, propaganda, in turn, had no direction and no purpose.

In summary, the first decision is to become a propaganda party; the next step is to have an idea that can be used for propaganda purposes, followed by propaganda itself. The idea and propaganda are intertwined and mutually dependent.

Suppose a new movement looks for interests to represent according to classical party logic. This has far-reaching consequences: such a movement will represent a social group—but has to oppose all others. For example, in the Weimar Republic, the nationalists had the liberals and the communists against them, as well as other competing nationalists. In this crowded spectrum, anyone who tried to unite as many voters as possible would have limited themselves enormously by concentrating on one social group.

The journalist and sociologist Siegfried Kracauer was already impressively precise about this in the mid-1930s. In "Totalitarian Propaganda," Kracauer explains Hitler's approach: "He cannot have the intention of making himself the party of some one-sided interests and thus of making National Socialism a party alongside the others."[1] The political cake had already been divided. Only niches remained. Thus, if one aimed for absolute power like Hitler, special interest politics were utterly counterproductive, no matter the cost. Interest politics would be a trap, a dead end. Thus, it was clear,

Kracauer wrote of Hitler, "that what mattered to him was not the defense of interests but the influencing of the masses, regardless of their interests."[2]

In the logic of a propaganda party, Hitler could not and did not want to place himself in the existing party spectrum with his new idea under any circumstances— as it would be just one of many. He had to put himself *above* the existing party system. Or at least apart from it. In Hannah Arendt's words, he had to be "in principle outside the party system."[3] The idea had to be constructed more extensively than all existing ones. It was not allowed to lean on a single social interest and narrow itself ideologically. Only if it strictly refrained from doing so could it be attractive to supporters of all other parties.

Thus, the National Socialist German Workers' Party pretended to unite the divisive political currents within itself. This idea placed the Nazis—initially and for a while only in theory—above their competitors, whose struggle between right and left, above and below, suddenly seemed petty. Regarding ideas, the Nazis hovered above the pettiness of the "normal" party system. They brought "a synthesis to the marketplace of words that promised national unity," as Hannah Arendt put it.[4]

Promising national unity above all particular interests, class antagonisms, or revolutionary enmities, as an insistent counterpoint, as it were, was how Hitler translated the primary approach of a propaganda party into reality: in defiance of the recent loss of the First World War, the collapse of the empire, and the ideological and physical clash of the old nationalism with burgeoning socialism.

The idea also had to respond to an economic, social, or cultural crisis—real or imagined—to give it a high degree of urgency. In addition, the idea absolutely had to be connectable to society, to the masses, to actual conditions, and to as large a part of the collective memory and emotional state as possible. The new was not allowed to be *too* new. That would be too foreign, equivalent to overstraining, and would not bring the desired connection to the masses. This compelling propagandistic principle of connectivity made Hitler draw on the past.

Hitler wrote in *Mein Kampf* about the extraordinary role of propaganda concerning the political idea. Propaganda would have to "tirelessly see that an idea wins adherents." It should make them "inclined" to the movement. "Propaganda works the whole in the spirit of an idea and makes it ripe for the time when that idea will be victorious." It should "draw people across" or "make them insecure in their previous convictions." The task of propaganda was "the destruction of the existing state of affairs and the infiltration of this state of affairs with the new doctrine."[5]

Joseph Goebbels—after-1930 official propaganda chief of the NSDAP and later minister of propaganda—was also aware of the interdependent relationship between ideas and propaganda. He saw the task of propaganda as being "to win people over to an idea, so deeply, so vividly, that in the end they become addicted to it and can no longer get away from it."[6]

An idea is not only the first and everlasting focus for the propagandist. It is the most important of all. If it fails in positioning itself outside the establishment, the entire movement does not resonate with the populace. According to Kracauer, Nazi propaganda in the mid-1930s could be understood as "an undertaking aimed at dynamizing the rigid system within which it stands. Only by unhinging this system, dismantling its stable framework, and shaking up the debris does it gain the possibility of distinguishing itself and gaining influence."[7]

At the beginning of the 1930s, Hitler declared that his goal was to "bridge the differences between the bourgeoisie and the proletariat" and that he wanted to "achieve the inner unification of millions of people who were drifting apart."[8] Goebbels presented this political idea in propaganda terms: "The battle cries are heard everywhere, the Catholics, the Protestants, the Bavarians, the Prussians, the bourgeois, the proletarians. One must conclude that there are no Germans left in Germany."[9] The other parties had "set themselves up on our bleeding backs." The nation was wasting its strength internally, which was the "consequence of corrupt party politics."[10] So away with party diversity, representative democracy, and ultimately away with parliament. Away with contradictions, complexity, and debate. A central idea for the good of the community of the people. In the name of national unity.

So what do the contemporary political ideas of propaganda politicians look like?

24

Viktor Orbán offers an impressive example. He was one of the founders of the initially liberal Fidesz party. With the fall of communism, it had become part of Hungary's party spectrum. In February 1992, Orbán, the leader of the Fidesz parliamentary group, uttered sentences that, in retrospect, are quite remarkable: "We have consistently refused to fight in such a way that the pure are on one side, the wicked on the other, the patriots are on one side, the traitors on the other [. . .] The ethnonational idea, the populist policy, is opposed to liberalism."[11]

But when strife broke out in Fidesz, and the party suffered a bitter political defeat in 1994, the ambitious Orbán turned in on himself. Being the leader of a small 5-percent party was far from enough for him. His biographer, Paul Lendvai, believes what came next was a calculated maneuver to somehow get into power.[12] Orbán's political idea can only be understood as an act of restorative nostalgia. Hungary had been on the losing side of history since the mid-nineteenth century.[13] Orbán saw an opportunity to focus his political ambition entirely on the battered Hungarian soul. He followed the idea of breathing self-esteem back into Hungarians. It was to be Us. Us against Them. Them could be Russia, the European Union, Merkel, or migrants. In this logic, Orbán now spoke of the home land and of Magyarism, which has its roots in the tenth century. He put national interests above everything, prayed publicly, and praised Christianity and the fatherland. Orbán thus left the level of separate interests and moved Fidesz out of the existing party spectrum.

In the 1998 parliamentary elections, Fidesz achieved 28.4 percent of the vote, and Orbán became Hungary's prime minister for his first four-year term. Since 2010, he has ruled with large majorities; in April 2022, he had around 53 percent. Islamophobia and anti-Semitism have taken hold: Fidesz has long used the entire bag of tricks of a pre-totalitarian propaganda party.

Another prominent example is the political idea of Turkey's Recep Tayyip Erdoğan. For a long time, Erdoğan was rooted in political Islam. His party, the Welfare Party, Refah Partisi, operated within the party system. But when Erdoğan was imprisoned in the late 1990s for reciting an Islamist poem, he developed an overarching idea for a new party, the AKP, based on Islam, westernization, economics, and prosperity. Erdoğan thus placed the AKP above the existing party system. In November 2002, just two and a half months after its foundation, the AKP won 34.3 percent of the votes in a landslide. Under pressure, Erdoğan later abandoned the more liberal, conciliatory reform course and played the Islamist-nationalist propaganda card on a massive scale to stay in power.

Turkey's neighbor, Greece, has a left-wing propaganda party, Syriza, which rose meteorically under its leader Alexis Tsipras during the grueling years of the euro debt crisis and bailouts. The far-left alliance that gave birth to Syriza in the years before had stood at 3 to 5 percent. The transformation into a party in 2012 boosted Syriza. Tsipras took over as president and formed a robust propaganda party in the following months and years. In May 2012, it climbed to

16.8 percent in the parliamentary elections and even to 26.9 percent in the subsequent elections six weeks later. During the election campaign, Tsipras used the slogan "Us against them"—a typical slogan for a propaganda party. Tsipras used the debt crisis, which had put Greece under extreme pressure within the European community for years, to make his mark. His political idea was based on uniting the Greeks against this external pressure and awakening their spirit of resistance. Nothing would do more to promote this in Greece's collective memory than a historical harking back to the resistance against the German conquerors of the Wehrmacht and Waffen-SS in the Second World War. In those years, the Nazis carried out the worst atrocities and bloodbaths in Greece. Workers had been the main resisters, but the whole population had suffered from war crimes and repression. Syriza insinuated this and called their opponents "Germanotsoliades," the name given to Greek Nazi collaborators in the Second World War. Alleged traitors to Greece were called the "fifth column of Germany." Syriza also referenced "occupying forces."[14] Many will remember Greek protests and posters showing German Chancellor Merkel with a Hitler mustache and wearing an SS uniform. The media picked up on the motif, and resentment was aroused. Mobilizing with this maximally accessible, emotionally charged message and language was a propagandistic success. It led Syriza out of the left corner. In 2015, Syriza won the most votes, well over 30 percent. Tsipras became prime minister. In 2019, Syriza was voted out of office but still held on to over 30 percent.

The political idea also played a central role in the rise and (temporary) fall of the forty-fifth president of the United States. Donald Trump's narcissistic message was "the political idea is me." He placed his person above the party system from the very beginning. He heaped contempt and insults on the Democrats, to whom he was once said to be partial. During the election campaign, he made his supporters chant, "Lock her up," meaning his opponent Hillary Clinton should go to jail. And he was not squeamish about "his" Republicans either. Instead, Trump attacked the entire US political elite. His battle cry, "Drain the swamp," made it abundantly clear—the swamp of Washington should be dried up. The "Trump Revolution," as investigative author Michael Wolff calls it in his bestseller *Fire and Fury*, "has always been about the weaknesses of the two major parties."[15] The fact Trump himself has been part of the country's elite all his life was evaded by a rhetorical trick. Because he belonged to it, he knew exactly what was happening. Trump had renounced the elites to serve only the people. With this story, he staged himself as a perceived outsider standing up for other perceived outsiders.

Trump would say phrases like, "I alone can fix things." or "Only I can solve the problem of radical Islamic terrorism."[16] One against all—Trump's political idea seems to come from one of the *Rambo* films, in which the hero practically incapacitates an entire Soviet army single-handedly, on horseback with a bow and arrow. Trump projected himself as the incarnation of revenge and reckoning. He served himself up as a projection screen for anger of every kind, which he would absorb and transport on social media, in return for loyalty at the ballot box. With this grandiose and furiously constructed political shell of the Rambo-like martyr, he would show them all. With this approach, Trump survived the primaries, won the presidential election, and stayed in office for four years.

The founding of the AfD (Alternative für Deutschland) in Germany initially had no propagandistic basis. They did include the signal term "alternative" in the party's name. But the political idea of the AfD did fit into the system. Euro-critical, pro-business, liberal-conservative: a cross between the economic wing of the FDP and the value-conservative wing of the CDU. The AfD, led by economics professor Bernd Lucke and ex-Siemens manager Hans-Olaf Henkel, wanted to bring back the deutsche mark—and abolish the euro and dissolve the monetary union in an orderly fashion. In 2013, the AfD failed to reach more than 5 percent of the national vote, thereby not qualifying to enter the German parliament (Bundestag). But it achieved its first success in 2014 with a little over 7 percent in the European elections. Thus, the AfD took a piece of the pie. It had positioned a political idea as a propaganda party, but it did not behave like one. Not yet.

For that to happen, first Frauke Petry had to defeat Lucke in the election for the chair in the summer of 2015. When that happened, the economic liberal wing dissolved. The German nationalist wing became the party's core, especially in eastern Germany. In September 2015, the so-called refugee crisis began, something party leader Alexander Gauland called a "gift." From the cynical point of view of a propaganda politician, it was this: the existing political idea was catapulted by this significant event into the center of society, freed from the veneer of particular interest of national conservative or ethnic ghosts. Merkel's decision to keep the border open for refugees allowed the AfD to become a propaganda party. The social media machine was ready and took off. There was no topic on which the AfD's key players had formed a more firm and unified opinion.

Quickly they could go on the attack and become the first stop for fears, frustration, and anger. Suddenly the term "alternative" suggested the party stood outside the system, something it knew how to fuel vigorously with jargon such as "legacy parties." The word "alternative" had a political boom and unquestionably hit the zeitgeist in terms of propaganda. By the 2017 federal election, the AfD was on a steep upward trajectory, improving by almost 8 percentage points to 12.6 percent.

In December 2016, the AfD leadership wrote a manifesto describing the AfD's strategy for the 2017 election year. It states the AfD comes "from the heart of the society." It is the one political force in the country that has the "courage to tell the truth," and its members "openly express their opinions." It picks up on the discontent of many citizens and gives them a voice:

"Conservatives, liberals and social democrats, and former nonvoters disappointed by the legacy parties find a home here. AfD politicians are not 'right-wing' or 'left-wing' but committed to reason and competence."

However, the manifesto continues, the AfD must distinguish itself more clearly from the far right, given "most voters self-identify in the political center." Furthermore, the AfD saw the greatest potential for more growth in the middle class among liberal conservatives. Therefore, it was important not to scare them away; radical demands should be well-founded and presented objectively. Moreover, the AfD was to be sold to the center and middle classes as the greatest "democratic project of the last decades" because the AfD had brought large numbers of nonvoters back to the polls.[17] This is precisely how a propaganda party positions itself. It claims to be there for everyone but excludes millions, especially migrants. It thinks it is electable for all classes—but has clear preferences. The AfD is highly ideological but pretends to be nonideological because supporters of the traditional parties, CDU/CSU, SPD, and FDP, could find a home here. In this way, the AfD acts to escape the corset of the left-right template. It simply declares itself to be at the center of society. It is far to the right but claims not to be. It has radical ideas but presents them as normal. The important thing is not to alienate anyone in the middle. This is what the "dynamization of the rigid system"—which Kracauer wrote about in the mid-1930s—looked like in early twenty-first-century Germany.

Two and a half years later, in the summer of 2019,

the AfD formulated another secret-strategy paper that, according to newspaper reports, reads like a seamless continuation. By 2025, the party wants to become a people's party and achieve at least 20 percent of votes nationwide. In the future, the party seeks to appeal even more to the conservative-liberal middle classes in the political center. To achieve this, certain image problems must be overcome.[18]

Image problems—a quaint way of framing the fact that the Office for the Protection of the Constitution (Verfassungsschutz) designated the ever-more-powerful branch of the AfD, "Der Flügel" (the Wing), as right-wing extremists and classified them as "suspect." In April 2020, Björn Höcke's "wing" was placed under observation (and formally dissolved a short time later). Less than a year after, the same office classified the entire AfD as suspected of right-wing extremism. The AfD took legal action against this, lost, and appealed. The case is still pending.[19]

The AfD's drift to the far right demonstrates that propaganda parties can fail to remain at the vote-getting core of a political idea. For the moment, the AfD has not succeeded. In its heyday, it stood outside the party system as a functioning, effective propaganda party. Still, it began playing too much to the right-wing fringe and thus positioned itself on the extreme right. As a result, in the 2021 federal election, it lost more than one million votes.[20] In state elections, it lost votes over the next two and a half years. In Lower Saxony, however, the AfD managed to almost double its vote in the fall of 2022 to 10.9 percent. Such swings in the will of the voters make it clear that no one can foresee whether the AfD has been permanently eliminated as an effective propaganda party.

One thing must be emphasized: the political idea is the nucleus of the propaganda party. It is shaped by the propagandists in such a way that it places the party above or beside—in any case, outside—the party system. The entire propaganda party stands and falls with the political idea. Only a good idea can be activated propagandistically.

Chapter 3

Corroding the Norms of Communication

With its political idea, the propaganda party has positioned itself outside the party spectrum. From there, it wants to attract as many voters as possible to gain or maintain power. Suppose the political idea is based on the harsh rejection of political competition. In that case, the propagandist's appearance and behavior have a guiding principle. Within this logic, propaganda politicians must conduct themselves as consistently as possible. The core message is this: we are like you, not like them. If the idea is anti-elitist, the propaganda politicians must also embody this.

In 2018, Harvard professors Steven Levitsky and Daniel Ziblatt, in their celebrated book *How Democracies Die*, used a political science perspective to show how the Republicans in particular—but not only them—had been undermining stable political norms and long-standing unwritten laws in the United States. This process started happening insidiously in the 1990s. The norms of political competition were replaced by those of political hostility. Simultaneously, the standard of mutual respect and tolerance was also abandoned. And the culture of compromise was replaced by rigid blockade politics. The deeply rooted culture of institutional restraint was abandoned to use every available political lever. Moreover, the authority of the elected president was called into question, starting in Obama's case with the claim that he was not American. There is no need to elaborate on how much President Trump has damaged the norm of respect for independent media and their role in the democratic process.[1]

Levitsky and Ziblatt highlighted four indicators of authoritarian behavior: rejecting (or feebly agreeing with) the rules of democracy; denying the legitimacy of political opponents; tolerating or encouraging violence; and being willing to curtail the civil liberties of opponents, including the media.[2]

In this book, I shall endeavor to add a critical component to the political analysis of these norms' erosion. As in politics, there are also unwritten laws in communication that shape democracies. But, in addition to political norms, propagandists also deliberately break communication norms. In their eyes, the more they break, the better. And the more often, the more effective.

Let's take the norm of issue-oriented communication. Most politicians communicate in a fact-oriented way. A striking example of this can be found in the case of Armin Laschet, then German CDU candidate for chancellor, who in the summer of 2021 said what he intended to do in the first hundred days after a possible election victory. The headline read: "Laschet: Plan acceleration will be the focus in first 100 days." The first sentence that followed was this: "Candidate for chancellor Armin Laschet wants to start by speeding up project planning and approval procedures in Germany if he takes over the government after the Bundestag elections." He would make "project plan acceleration packages a priority."[3] Here, a politician describes what grievance he sees, says he wants to remedy it, and outlines an approach to a solution. It could hardly be more fact oriented. This example shows that fact-oriented communication can be small-scale because politics is. It is pointless to ponder whether a propaganda politician would communicate this way.

Propaganda politicians break this norm of fact-oriented communication in every imaginable way. They engage in highly person-centered communication. When they are not talking about themselves, their communication is laced with constant attacks on political competitors or people in the public sphere, especially those who stand for a different opinion. That is why German AfD politician Alexander Gauland's statement about the newly reelected Chancellor Merkel, "We will hunt her down," had a powerful impact. It was a breach of norms. Donald Trump's invective against his political opponents is etched in our minds. Erdoğan's "Sen kimsin?"—"Who are you?"—toward the opposition leader has become a catchphrase in Turkey. Viktor Orbán has used his communications to make George Soros an enemy of the state. The list of such attacks is long.

Let us zoom in from communication in general to the specifics of language, and the next unwritten norm that propagandists like to violate becomes apparent. We can call it the norm of moderation in speech. Democratic politicians essentially negotiate issues using moderate, deliberative, and factual language. Propagandist language, on the other hand, usually attacks and is harsh, derogatory, and not infrequently dehumanizing. Propagandists goad their audience. They pursue a tactic of linguistic vehemence. They pretend as though the excitement of the masses has been transferred to them, as though they are part of the masses and are only expressing what the masses feel and want. They represent what has become known as the "felt truth." They give validation to their supporters. This unspoken message of ideological affiliation is part of propaganda politicians' deliberate use of language.

That this is a deliberate tactic is shown by an internal strategy paper of the AfD from 2017, which states: "The AfD must [. . .] be quite deliberately politically incorrect, resort to clear words, and not shy away from carefully planned provocations." And further: "The reactions and sensitivities of other sections of society are of secondary importance for the AfD [. . .]. They are targets rather than constituencies of the AfD."[4]

For propaganda politicians, deliberately not speaking like other politicians is a virtue. Talking like someone from the street is best if you want to conquer the street. You keep proving that you can speak like them: simple, straightforward, and tough.

It has often been described that language can dehumanize, lower inhibitions, and encourage acts of violence when, for example, terms like "freeloaders" and "parasites" or references to diseases and filth of all kinds are used in connection with people. Nevertheless—or precisely because of this—such linguistic escalation can be observed repeatedly among propaganda politicians. Putin, for example, called demonstrators "squeaking monkeys" and terrorists he wanted to "destroy like rats"; Trump called his political competitors, among other things, "human scum"[5]; German politician Gauland wanted to "deport the social democratic integration commissioner to Anatolia."

More sophisticated than the sledgehammer method of calculated linguistic derailment is the use of framing according to Hebb's learning rule. The psychologist Donald Olding Hebb established this rule in 1949. His neurophysiological findings are summarized in the phrase "what fires together, wires together." In other words, if I constantly associate two terms with each other, the brain will remember them together. In principle, this is how vocabulary learning works. However, this learning mechanism can also be misused. Propaganda politicians deliberately bring pairs of terms together: Jews and conspirators, Muslims and terrorists, Mexicans and rapists, crooked and Hillary, sleepy and Joe. Crucial in this context is that negatory statements become irrelevant to the brain. If someone in a debate makes the correct and classifying statement, "Only very few Muslims are terrorists," the brain still remembers the link between Muslims and terrorists. Propaganda politicians and their online brigades attach great importance to these patterns. They observe them and actively try to trigger them—by setting framing traps for their political opponents. This also includes disparaging the press, the competition, or the courts as "leftist filth."

Propaganda politicians then create dehumanizing or derogatory fighting terms—their own vocabulary and code, which supporters immediately recognize. Many words became established in Germany during the Nazi era and have since been used repeatedly; propaganda does not have to be particularly imaginative if the tried and tested still works. Political consultant Johannes Hillje, like others, already pointed out that today's propaganda in Germany often recycles Nazi vocabulary. "Lying press" is a term that Goebbels, Hitler, and the Nazi leadership used repeatedly. "Legacy parties" was coined by the Nazis, and the term "puppets" is a staple of propaganda vocabulary across the ages. Hitler first introduced the accusation of treason against the people and then spoke of "traitors to the people" and "enemies of the people." Such terms today are part of propaganda 101, frequently used in all kinds of countries, not only in Germany but also in Great Britain, Turkey, and the United States. This language code also serves to simplify. It reinforces the "simple truths" of right and wrong, up and down, them and us. "Traitor to the people" or "enemy of the people," for example. "Enemy of the people" is a catch-all term into which all kinds of enemies can be classified and pushed: other parties, institutions, media, or individuals, for example. This provides the desired propagandistic simplification and produces the maximum effect, especially since individuals can interpret for themselves who they consider enemies of the people. Hitler declared in a speech in 1925 that the masses were incapable of focusing on several enemies at once. "It is part of the genius of a great leader to make even opponents who are separate always appear to belong to only one category."[6]

If we zoom out from concrete language, another important dimension comes into view. This is the norm of metacommunicative integration. Political debates and conflicts are often judged—in the situation as well as in retrospect—according to who was right, who prevailed, and who won. As controversial and harsh as some political debates that produce those victors may be, the strife becomes irrelevant within the norm of metacommunicative integration. Instead, this norm directs attention to a level superordinate to communication—metacommunication. On this level, the mode of communicative action is considered. The protagonists' ability to enable and endure an exchange of viewpoints, arguments, and proposed solutions is evaluated. According to this standard, a debate that allows the audience to perceive and accept existing interpretations has a particular value, for it produces a diversity of perspectives. The political protagonists thus exemplify a culture of debate and the ability to deal with conflict, which has a socially integrating effect because it strives for agreement.

There is hardly a norm that propagandists break as fundamentally as this one. Their anti-norm is metacommunicative polarization. The point is that it is almost impossible to enter dialogue with "hostile" competition. Such is the real message when journalists are excluded from party rallies, media representatives are branded as undesirable at White House press conferences, or talk shows are demonstratively exited. This phenomenon has already reached the private and personal spheres. Be it about the refugee issue, COVID-19, or compulsory vaccination. "There's no talking to him anymore"—this statement has led to the disintegration of friendships and the irreconcilable breakdown of relationships.

Breaking the norm of metacommunicative integration has now achieved maximum effectiveness. For some time now, polarization has been one of the most discussed topics at many levels of society. The primary root of this polarization lies in precisely this breached norm of metacommunicative integration. And it is a component that the propagandists carefully emphasize—embedded in and condensed by the other strategies already cited here. These examples show how political ideas are affirmed outside the party system by breaking communicative norms. From the point of view of the propaganda strategist, this creates a very coherent image: "We are different. You can experience that at every level, in every facet of us. So we must be different." This coherence gives rise to credibility and trust among the electorate.

Finally, there is one last important norm propaganda breaks with. This norm influences the attitude with which actors enter political discourse in the first place. The American linguist Adam Hodges, who analyzed Trump's communication, points to research in the 2000s that showed people have a "truth bias."[7] We initially assume other people are telling the truth. We take a leap of faith. Accordingly, Hodges argues, there can be a "discourse of truthfulness" that strives for as much objectivity as possible. Hodges contrasts this desirable, normative discourse with the "discourse of theater" Trump engages in. Distortion of truth takes hold, which is why many people are willing to engage with Trump in the first place. In this theater world, politics are pure drama, full of messages designed to appeal to the emotional cravings of the target audience. Language and communication here serve to "convey emotion and appeal to the politician's general ideological orientation rather than specific policy details."[8]

This should give all observers pause. Trump may have taken the discourse of theater to a temporary extreme. Still, it can easily be transferred to other countries. There is little room for fact-based communication in the discourse of theater. Truthfulness plays no role. Worse still, it is not needed at all.

Chapter 4

Conspiracy Allegations: The Framework of Manipulative Reinterpretation

We have been telling each other so-called conspiracy theories for a long time. Wikipedia even has a list that goes back to the twelfth century. Here you will find alleged ritual murders, the poisoning of wells, and witchcraft—as well as the mother of modern conspiracy theories, which claims there is a secret circle of Jews who control the world's fate. The *Protocols of the Wise Men of Zion* were circulated in the second half of the nineteenth century. The historian Wolfgang Benz traced how these wafted through Europe. Hitler and Goebbels considered them untrue, but the Nazis picked them up anyway—always mindful of their propagandistic potential.[1]

Today, conspiracy theories are booming—both in terms of quantity and prevalence and in terms of attempts to explain the phenomenon. There is a bouquet of conspiracy theories, from malicious reptilian humanoids to so-called chemtrails to highly political approaches such as the claim that the US government itself carried out the 9/11 terrorist attacks. A whole series of bizarre conspiracy theories has been added around coronavirus.

To approach the phenomenon, we should first clarify the terminology because, strictly speaking, these are not theories. The term "conspiracy theories" lends an entirely wrong impression of being scientific. The same applies to the term "conspiracy hypotheses." Nor are they myths that would have cultural value because of their long tradition. "Conspiracy ideology" narrows the view to the overarching assessment and ignores the fundamental question of truth content. The now more commonly used term "conspiracy narratives" also distracts from the essential: the point is not, after all, that real conspiracies are being told or narrated. If we want as soberly and value-neutral a term as possible, then "conspiracy allegations" seems more appropriate. The claim is the existence of unbelievable and incredibly large-scale conspiracies.

The discussion about conspiracy allegations includes the broad field of lies and truth. Are conspiracy claims simply lies? Many will see them that way—or regard some of them as folk superstition. On the other hand, propagandists and conspiracy believers have been quick to bolster their claims with supposed evidence and a plethora of details. In addition, these "proofs" and details are supposed to challenge all other narratives: the conspiracy claim sows doubt. "Prove me wrong!" is a standard line of argument. Anyone who engages out of a desire to enlighten enters the propagandist's arena and must be aware of this. To better understand conspiracy allegations, it is crucial to focus on their deeper functional content, for therein lies hidden the remarkable effectiveness of conspiracy allegations.

A particularly effective conspiracy allegation has been doing the rounds in Europe since the beginning of this millennium. It alleges that the European elites want to exchange their Christian citizens for Muslims through a "great repopulation." Many propaganda parties resort to this claim, which originated in the book *Le grand remplacement* by the French neo-right-winger Renaud Camus.

Donald Trump and his entourage are directly responsible for various conspiracy claims and their dissemination, such as the claim that Barack Obama was not born in the United States and thus his election was illegitimate. Trump had put himself at the head of the "birther" movement well before he ran for office. At the end of his presidency, Trump built up his most consequential conspiracy allegation by claiming he was ousted by fraud and a stolen election.

All this is, of course, nonsense. Propagandist conspiracy allegations are destructive fabrications of reality, complex constructs of lies with the sole aim of subliminal manipulation. There is still shock at how people can fall for these fabrications. And yet, regarding propaganda parties, it is important not to dismiss this issue, because we would otherwise fail to properly understand the propagandistic function and effect. We must consider psychological phenomena such as the various forms of cognitive distortion ("bias") that our brains engage in. The belief in conspiracy allegations also has rationally tangible functions: it makes sense of a chaotic world, it creates a feeling of control where there is a perception of loss of power, and it reinforces the self-image of the believer because they believe they have a better grasp of matters than others—that they belong to those in the know who have an understanding of things.[2] The others are devalued as thoughtless and asleep, which, to continue the historical parallel with the Nazis, is not coincidentally reminiscent of the Nazi slogan "Deutschland erwache" ("Germany awake"), a phrase frequently found on Nazi banners.

At this point, the focus should be on the communicative context of propaganda and conspiracy beliefs, which has been under-explored and barely debated systematically so far.[3] Allegedly, there is no connection between propaganda and conspiracy allegations. Conspiracy thinking is a "nonessential element of populist discourse,"[4] that is to say, of propagandist discourse. But this research overlooks a very fundamental aspect of propaganda. As will become apparent in the following pages, there is very much a close, even a necessary and compelling, connection. After the political idea has been conceived and underpinned by the breach of communication norms, every subsequent step by the propaganda party must generate maximum engagement. This is the be-all and end-all because, without engagement, there is no chance of stirring. Without that, there will be no followers. To this end, the originality and uniqueness of the enterprise must be proven to the audience. The abstract idea must also be framed in a narrative to generate attention. It needs a simple, catchy, and thus memorable translation into people's lives. People are very good at translating abstraction into substance with the help of stories.

From time immemorial, people have been storytellers and listeners—through oral tradition or cave painting. Stories are potent conveyors of information and emotion. There has never been a period in human history in which so many people have told so many stories as in our time. Stories are being told more professionally than ever. And they are being told through so many channels: on radio and television stations, on social media, in self-published books, in the cinema, in streaming platforms' shows, in the audio sector, and in self-portrayals by individuals or organizations. There can hardly have ever been a generation more intensely practiced in consuming and absorbing masses of stories than the current generation. The media saturation of the present is unsurpassed. The amount of data uploaded to YouTube alone breaks records year after year. Narratives are omnipresent. So much is wrapped up in stories. Good versus evil is one of the oldest motifs in human history, and it dominates many narratives today.

As a result, people nowadays have exceptionally well-trained narrative and receptive muscles. And our memories—our hard drives for stories—are pretty full. So you must tell an extraordinary, gripping narrative to be noticed.

Attention is an essential aspect of conspiracy allegations. A propaganda party can achieve the greatest effect on issues that have not yet had media visibility. The approach, therefore, involves opening new playing fields in which the propagandist a) determines the rules of the game, b) is dominant in terms of content, and c) is sure to get media attention. A propaganda party that places itself outside the mainstream must also pick up stories from outside the mainstream—or at least pretend to do so consistently. Conspiracy allegations are some of the most powerful stories that circulate outside the mainstream and have usually "stood the test of time" over many years because they have been able to engage numerous people. Therefore, the use or construction of conspiracy allegations is highly useful for propaganda parties.

Viewed through the lens of communication experts, conspiracy allegations can be understood as large interpretive frames, which shall be referred to as meta-frames in the following. Framing, in this context, means a deliberate choice of words or topics that provide an interpretive framework in which a matter is discussed. Every (political) story can be subject to a conscious choice of words and themes. The "meta" is meant to indicate the size of the interpretive frame—many political conspiracy allegations are extensive. As a result, a lot can be read into them and docked onto them. This, in turn, is enormously important for a propaganda party because it can frame everyday occurrences within the context of the alleged conspiracy and use them as "evidence." Those who want to invalidate this "evidence" are already playing the propagandist's and conspiracy believer's game and are starting from the defensive. Any rebuttal generates additional attention for the original propaganda—an intractable dilemma.

Meta-frames function as reinterpretation tools. Linking as many individual events as possible to the overarching macro-assertion of the conspiracy keeps fueling the theme anew. It condenses the issue, imprints it on the masses, and produces credibility among the receptive public that makes the connection. Meta-frames form anchor points amid a news cycle that is constantly in motion. They act like magnets for public attention.

Let's take the conspiracy allegation of repopulation as an example. The political elite wants to replace its people with Muslims, so the scenario goes. If German Chancellor Scholz now appoints a politician of Muslim faith to replace a Christian predecessor, the propaganda party will most likely place this event within the framework of the conspiracy allegation of *Umvolkung* (repopulation). It does not take much imagination to conjure other events that fit into this framework and supposedly "prove" the conspiracy allegation.

Another scenario: Chancellor Merkel allows many refugees into the country. In that case, this is framed as having nothing to do with humanitarianism but—clearly—with the meta-frame of repopulation. "Anchor heuristics" come into play here: placing the event quickly and aggressively within this interpretative framework sets the anchor point for further discussion. The playing field is marked out. The other parties have to chip away at the tall theses of the propaganda party. It is no coincidence that propaganda parties are the best purveyors of the attention economy. They use, whenever possible, the media power of the first strike.

Two psychological facts massively facilitate this instrument of conspiracy allegations as meta-frames for everyday political agitation. First, the US sociologist Ted Goertzel discovered in the mid-1990s that people who believe in one conspiracy allegation strongly tend to accept others at face value.[5] This means that only one conspiracy allegation has to resonate with a person. It's like a gateway drug, and the entire field of conspiracy belief is unlocked. That's also probably why there are so many conspiracy allegations: so that people with different fears and convictions can be hooked and thus made accessible for propaganda work. Moreover, the meta-frames based on a conspiracy allegation are subject to confirmation bias. Psychologist Peter Wason identified this cognitive bias already in the 1960s. People prefer to take in information that confirms their existing opinion. If I believe in a conspiracy allegation, the corresponding data will reach me exceptionally well, and I will also believe it—which strengthens my opinion. Once successfully seeded and persistently nurtured, these meta-frames can be triggered around the clock—unless opinion leaders, for example, in the social networks—create the links themselves and set the agenda. In this case, the propaganda party only needs to ride the wave. In professional communications, we call this "agenda surfing." The flexibility of linking events with a conspiracy allegation within a meta-frame should not be underestimated, because a wide variety of conspiracy allegations are being circulated, and more can be formed at a moment's notice. New topics, such as COVID-19 vaccination, can also emerge. The success of this strategy can be measured and documented in real time, especially on social media.

Examining self-set conspiracy allegations by propaganda parties can be very revealing. A four-stage narrative pattern becomes discernible:

1. First, an allegedly scandalous event is identified, or an intolerable situation is highlighted.
2. In the next step, the culprits are denounced.
3. An approaching dystopia is described.
4. Finally, immediate action is claimed to be necessary to defend the country or to save the world.

The following example from the United States shows what this matrix looks like in concrete cases:

1. A once-powerful America is decaying. We can't even protect our borders from rapists and criminals coming into our country illegally.
2. It's the fault of the detached, weak elite in Washington who let these criminals into the country.
3. If we do nothing, our country will soon collapse.
4. We must rise now before it is too late.

Donald Trump used this conspiracy allegation narrative to gain the presidency. In the summer of 2022, Dick Morris, a political adviser to Trump, presented a 230-page book in which he outlined the message that would enable the Republican to get back into office.[6] This vividly illustrates how alive and present the patterns of thought and techniques described are. Propaganda is here and now. It is fermenting in dozens of places worldwide at this very moment.

Morris's idea of a conspiracy allegation can be summarized in terms of the 2024 presidential election:

1. The US is in danger of becoming a colony of China, which means the end of our freedoms and way of life.
2. The culprits are President Biden, who is on China's payroll, and the radical, Marxist, revolutionary backers in the Democratic Party using Biden as a puppet.
3. If no one steps in immediately, we will become economically dependent on China, we will have racial segregation against whites, we will drown in a sea of illegal immigration, and environmental fantasists will remodel the US so that we—the majority—will no longer be able to recognize our own country.
4. Donald Trump must be elected president in 2024 because he has already succeeded once in awakening America's sleeping center; he is the only one who can prevent America's demise.

In the UK, the conspiracy allegation narrative that underpinned the Brexit campaign ran as follows:

1. We are losing our national autonomy and identity.
2. Blame it on our fearful leadership, which is bowing to the dictates of the EU, which Germany dominates.
3. If nothing is done, EU bureaucrats will soon take over our country and take our money out of our pockets.
4. We must leave the EU immediately to save our country from ruin.

The conspiracy allegation of repopulation has already been introduced. It is being told in Germany, Austria, France, and Hungary like this:

1. There is a repopulation going on, hence all the uncontrolled immigration.
2. It's the fault of the multicultural puppets in our governments (in the EU or at the United Nations, which George Soros and other backers control).
3. If nothing happens, they will take our country away from us.
4. We must close the borders now and kick out the Muslims. Otherwise, our country as we know it is doomed.

Even the conspiracy allegation of the Nazis, which had catastrophic consequences, worked along the same lines:

1. The world conspired against Germany. Just look at the Treaty of Versailles.
2. The Jews and the Bolsheviks (who are infiltrated by Jews) are to blame. They control the German government.
3. If nothing is done, we will be destroyed for good.
4. We must defend our country by any means before it's too late.

We can see that these conspiracy allegations are constructed in the same way. They are full of negative energy but good at "dynamizing the rigid system." The narratives are simple:

1. Everything is already certain and transparent.

2. The case is solved.
3. The culprits are effortlessly identified because they are extraordinarily incompetent and defenseless, despite their apparent cunning and enormous goals.[7]

Any real complexity is explained away, and good and evil are marked. The saviors of the propaganda party are ready. The hero only has to act . . . .

Each stage of this mechanism demands to be constructed propagandistically:

1. Scandalous event or intolerable state of affairs: Propaganda needs a significant threat as a starting point. The greater, the better. The stakes are high. Our very existence is at risk.
2. The culprits: Propaganda must ensure the culprits are named but also described vaguely. The best way is to latch on to existing resentments.
3. Approaching dystopia: The doomsday scenario must be drastic. Critical. We are under attack. We are forced to react in self-defense. We are, without a doubt, morally in the right, which legitimizes the adoption of drastic measures.
4. Immediate action: The urgency must become apparent. Hence propaganda politicians keep intoning the "it's almost midnight" rhetoric. It is comparable to the call to action in the advertising industry, that the advertisement is only meant to make you buy a product. And, of course, only the leader of the propaganda party has the clout to master this huge problem.

The American scholar Michael Butter has studied numerous conspiracy allegations and discovered two parameters in their narrative patterns. While conspiracy allegations are always constructed in the same way, they differ in terms of where the alleged conspiracy originates: according to Butter, it can be triggered from below or from above and come from outside or from within.[8]

Let's look at these two parameters in the conspiracy allegations of propaganda parties striving for power. A consistent picture emerges: the alleged conspiracies here always come from outside and are fed from above. The ruling elite of the respective country is weak and incompetent. The real threat comes from Mexico, Islamic countries, or even the rest of the world. This combination—conspiracy from above and from outside—is, on closer examination, anything but a coincidence. If it were not the "outside" that was pilloried but the "inside," the public would be among the alleged conspirators. But it is that public the propaganda party wants to win over. And if the ruling elite "above" were not involved in the imagined conspiracy, it would be the task of those already in power to act against the grievance.

Thus, if propagandists must somehow win over the masses to replace the incumbent political elite and come to power for power's sake, this is the only feasible combination in constructing a conspiracy allegation driven by political interests. It can be reduced to this formula: conspiracy allegation equals a four-stage narrative pattern multiplied by conspiracy from outside and above. The propaganda party works precisely and flexibly with conspiracy allegations to make its idea as relatable as possible and to read all possible events into this frame of interpretation.

All in all, conspiracy allegations are imperative building blocks for manipulation, providing meta-frames for reinterpreting current events. And as various studies at the national and international levels consistently demonstrate, they are a highly successful component of the propaganda toolbox. The biennial Leipzig Authoritarianism Study[9] came to these core findings for Germany around the end of 2020:

1. In the pandemic, conspiracy mentality rose to 38.4 percent (in 2018, it was 30.8 percent).
2. Almost one in three people think most others do not realize the extent to which secret conspiracies determine our lives—and that politicians are only puppets of the powers behind them.
3. Over 38 percent agree that secret organizations greatly influence political decisions.

But conspiracy allegations are only one building block of several that impact the terrain of lies and truth.

Chapter 5
Big Lies

In the communications logic of propaganda parties, lies play a prominent role, which is why they are considered separately here. Adolf Hitler already dealt extensively with lies as a political tool. He did so openly and bluntly. Various reflections on this can be found in *Mein Kampf.*[1]

He attached particular importance to the big lie: "All this was inspired by the principle—which is quite true in itself—that in the big lie, there is always a certain force of credibility because the broad masses of a nation are always more easily corrupted in the deeper strata of their emotional nature than consciously or voluntarily, and thus in the primitive simplicity of their minds, they more readily fall victims to the big lie than the small lie."[2] He's saying weak-minded people would swallow a big lie more quickly than a small one because they could not even imagine such a big lie was possible. That was Hitler's logic.

The propagandists of the Nazi regime really did have an intuitive grasp of human nature. Decades later, research in social psychology established that proportionality bias could be observed in humans. In short, this means we believe that big events also have big causes. This is in us—and is of highly detrimental effectiveness, especially concerning big lies.

Hitler boasted that he had managed to pin his attempted coup on his partner Erich Ludendorff, a general and politician, thanks to a big lie. Lies run through the entire Nazi period. In 1938, regarding the question of the Sudetenland, he demanded "German" parts of Czechoslovakia. Hitler announced it was "the last territorial demand" he would make in Europe.[3] A year later, he attacked Poland and triggered the Second World War. These cases can be categorized as outright lies.

In this context, conspiracy allegations are nothing more than blatant falsehoods. And there is a third type of lie that is presented here because it was not only used massively by the Nazis but is also used intensively today. This lie was already called "mirror reflex" in the 1930s: you don't invent a bald-faced lie, but you turn the truth upside down and swap horse and rider. Siegfried Kracauer described this phenomenon very precisely at the time:

"One does not interpret the truth but rather twists it by [accusing] the opponent of exactly those actions and machinations that lie along one's lines—a much-observed maneuver that has been christened 'mirror reflex.'"[4]

Goebbels made ample use of this technique in his texts and articles. Especially concerning Jews, he twisted the roles of aggressor and victim repeatedly. For example, in his 1929 article "Der Jude," he wrote:

"Quickly, he turns the opponent into that which he actually wanted to fight in him: the liar, the mischief-maker, the terrorist. Nothing would be more wrong than to want to defend oneself against it. That is what the Jew wants. He then invents new lies every day, against which his opponent must now defend himself. He does not get to what the Jew is actually afraid of: attacking him. The accused has now become the accuser and presses the accuser into the dock with much shouting."[5]

Goebbels describes what the Nazis did to the Jews and claims it was the other way around. Goebbels often used this brazen perpetrator-victim reversal, revealing his strategy but simply blaming it on his victims.

There are good reasons to detail the roots of the modern political lie in Nazi propaganda. It is imperative to know the concrete techniques and their origins to understand how contemporary propaganda operates. Especially the method of the mirror reflex should not be underestimated in its effect. Unlike outright lies, which have no connection with reality, the mirror reflex works by reversing reality. It correlates lies and truth by turning everything upside down. This is not a mothballed technique. Nowadays, we also speak of reverse labelling.[6]

Russian war propaganda has tried to justify the illegal war of aggression on Ukraine with a whole arsenal of lies. It justified the massive military presence on the border long before the war began, claiming Ukraine was planning a military offensive in Donbas. This can be called a spotless-mirror reflex. Until the beginning of the war, Russia claimed these were only troop exercises, that they had no other intentions and posed no danger. In addition to this outright lie, there was another mirror reflex: the West was conducting maneuvers in Ukraine. It was "alarming" how many troops Ukraine had amassed near the pro-Russian areas in eastern Ukraine. When the war began, Russia claimed it had been forced to invade, as it were, to protect its population in Donbas from genocide. Finally, Russia came up with the conspiracy allegation that the Ukrainian government was fascist and that Ukraine should be de-Nazified. The Nazi framing here was an attempt to score points on the home front by triggering proud memories of the victory in the Great Patriotic War. However, President Zelensky is Jewish. His grandfather served in the Soviet army as an officer in World War II, and his great-uncles and great-grandfather were murdered in the Holocaust.[7]

Propaganda is more cunning in the United States. Again, it is inevitable to cite Donald Trump as an example. Trump built a parallel world of "alternative facts" aimed solely at catering to the sensibilities of his followers and triggering emotions—with the goal of generating unquestioning allegiance. He has demonstrably set sad records. The *Washington Post*'s fact-checkers counted more than thirty thousand misleading claims and false statements by Trump during his presidency.[8]

Trump, by the way, adopted his casual relationship with the truth as a method decades before his political career. In his 1987 book, *The Art of the Deal*, he wrote:

"I play to people's fantasies. People may not always think big themselves, but they can still get very excited by those who do. That's why a little hyperbole never hurts. People want to believe that something is the biggest and the greatest, and the most spectacular. I call it truthful hyperbole. It's an innocent form of exaggeration—and a very effective form of promotion."[9]

The sales philosophy of "truthful exaggeration" must have taken on a life of its own in the years that followed.

When Trump ruled in office, he frequently used phrases like "I was told," "people are saying"; "I heard on TV" . . . followed by the wildest conspiracy allegations and lies. This is where it gets interesting. Because these phrases were no coincidence. First, they signaled to his followers that he was listening to them, even echoing them, and thus honoring them. In addition, and this aspect is not as obvious, the unassuming, colloquial addition was meant to provide more credibility. People do not like to believe a singular statement. It becomes more effective when several people join a statement and say the same thing. In the end, such a chain of authentication qualifies even dubious and nontransparent sources of origin for a statement because the source is blurred and superimposed by the supposedly conclusive chain. This phenomenon was discovered by the linguistic anthropologist Judith Irvine in her research on racism in the late 1980s.[10]

But the chain of authentication is not the only hidden function. The innocuous-seeming "I was told" has another purpose. The reference to an unspecified source provided the possibility for Trump to retract a statement, if necessary, without being harmed. He could say that, unfortunately, someone had told him something wrong. Therefore, in a flash, he is off the hook. There is also a technical term for this, which goes back to the times before Trump: plausible deniability.

Plausible deniability on the one hand and the chain of authentication on the other—the two functions of "I was told."

The functions of "I was told" only seem like a paradox at first glance. For a liar like Trump, they are perfect: maximized effect of the misleading statement—combined with the minimized danger of being held accountable. This is how Political Lie Spreading 4.0 works.

Mirror reflexes were as much part of President Trump's repertoire as outright lies. The biggest and most daring mirror reflex was the one that triggered an earthquake in the media world: "You are fake news." A notorious liar accuses journalists from the country's most respected media of lying. He calls his lies "alternative facts" and, in turn, labels scientifically recognized facts as lies. This is reminiscent—in the spirit of the discourse theater above—of Shakespeare's *Macbeth*: "Fair is foul, and foul is fair."

Trump and Putin are by no means the only contemporary propagandists working with outright lies and mirror reflexes. In Germany, for example, the AfD operates with the claim that a dictatorship of opinion rules the country. One can no longer speak one's mind. The mainstream has undermined freedom of expression. Yet the party and its supporters never leave anything unsaid. They were never prevented from speaking. Nothing was suppressed. Instead, the AfD and its sympathizers want to impose their opinion on the rest. They do not allow any other view to be valid and—especially on the Internet—shout down dissenters and encourage or approve of violent fantasies, violence, and, yes, even murder. A mirror reflex par excellence. Former chancellor Angela Merkel rightly noted that freedom of expression does not mean banning dissent.[11]

Another case in point is the propaganda of the PiS party in Poland. When, for example, a debate arose in Poland about the country's role during the Nazi era, it was summarily stated that "anti-Polish forces are plotting to blame Poland instead of Germany for Auschwitz."[12]

However, the PiS party works not only with simple lies but also with a complex web of conspiracy allegations. The biggest of these revolves around the crash of the presidential plane in 2010, in which the then-incumbent president Lech Kaczyński died. In a very short time, a conspiracy allegation was spread, especially by the deceased's twin brother, Jarosław Kaczyński. The historical context of the presidential trip spurred this. Lech Kaczyński was going to attend the commemoration of the seventieth anniversary of the Katyn massacre, in which Joseph Stalin had ordered the murder of twenty-one thousand Polish soldiers. Jarosław Kaczyński, in hints and outbursts of rage, originated the claim that the liberal-conservative government of Donald Tusk was in cahoots with the Russians and had murdered his brother. However, the official investigation using a black box revealed something entirely different. According to the report, there was fog over Smolensk in Russia. The pilots considered flying to another city. Kaczynski's team must have exerted pressure; the head of the air force encouraged the pilots to have the confidence to land in Smolensk. But there was no airport, only a forest landing strip. The plane hit some treetops, flipped over, and hit the ground. A tragic accident. Despite this, the PiS party has built up and maintained the conspiracy allegation about Smolensk.[13]

It is fair to ask why today's propaganda parties rely on outright lies. These days, statements can often be checked quickly; the media responded to the supposed post-factual age with more fact-checking. One thing is clear: lies entail considerable reputational risks. But this does not apply to supporters of the propaganda party. For them, lies confirm their worldview. Lies help propaganda politicians make themselves "like us" and create an emotional bond. The nonexistent factuality of the lies is irrelevant. What matters is the ideological credibility of the lie. The lie is a confidence-building measure for supporters. Immediately after the accident, one in ten believed in a conspiracy. A few years later, it was one in five.[14] The repetition of the lie is essential. Consider those for whom the lie doesn't already fit into their worldview, as it does with the followers. In that case, repetition makes them more familiar with the statement or assertion. Repetition makes a statement or claim sound familiar, making it more credible in our minds. Since the end of the 1970s, this has been referred to as the "illusory truth effect." This is not only true for people who are unsure of what is right or wrong. Even knowledge does not protect against the illusory truth effect. In 2015, a team of researchers led by Lisa K. Fazio found that even people who knew the actual correct facts changed their view by being repeatedly exposed to misinformation. The psychologists attributed this to the fact the brain memorized false information through repetition, and it was thus easier to recall. The brain misinterpreted this easier recall as truthfulness. The false statement overwrote the actual existing knowledge. In psychology, this phenomenon is called "processing fluency."[15] A follow-up study by Fazio showed that the illusory truth effect is likely to be universal and can already be demonstrated in five-year-olds.[16] If one widens the perspective further to target the entire population, it's clear the Nazis, as the fathers of modern propaganda, clearly understood why they worked with lies.

Hitler said, "It would never come into their heads to fabricate colossal untruths, and they would not believe that others could have the impudence to distort the truth so infamously. Even though the facts which prove this to be so may be brought clearly to their minds, they will still doubt and waver and will continue to think that there may be some other explanation.

For the grossly impudent lie always leaves traces behind it, even after it has been nailed down, a fact which is known to all expert liars in this world and to all who conspire together in the art of lying."[17]

To create this uncertainty, sinister communication work was needed to ensure it would stick. These statements reveal the propaganda chief of his party, which Hitler was in the beginning, coolly considering another instrument's advantages for his cause. Yes, even more in history and the present, every event was merely malleable putty if one had the power and callousness to reinvent it. Hannah Arendt described how the idea of "establishing lies, provided they are big and bold enough, as unquestionable facts" was tremendously seductive to the Nazis.[18]

History shows how history repeats itself. The propagandist logic of the lies of the Nazis was decoded in the mid-1930s by the already-quoted Siegfried Kracauer:

> "Their mission is to create an oscillation of lies and truth that denies their distinction, to bring the recipients of propaganda into the same confusion to which visitors to a hall of mirrors are subjected. The vertigo that seizes the masses forces them to close their eyes and put aside the question of the veracity of any propagandist thesis."[19]

The logic of the propagandist lie has been well-established for a long time. The Nazi regime showed its monstrous effects to the whole world in an unprecedented form. Living conditions have changed, education and knowledge have expanded, and Western democracy has succeeded. And despite all this, the propagandistic lie is still influential. Even more remarkable is how utterly helpless democratic parties have been and still are in dealing with their competition. How overwhelmed public opinion was and is in bringing light, on a broad front, into the present darkness.

Let's keep in mind that the oscillation of lies and truth confuses people. This confusion is supposed to make them no longer distinguish between lies and truth. They are supposed to abandon the endeavor entirely and perceive politics solely on the level of belief and feeling—the very level that is the absolute focus of every propaganda party, to which it directs its energy and its forces, on which it specializes. Through lies, voters are psychologically pushed onto the propagandist's playing field.

However, and this thought leads to the next chapter, there is much more to the lies of the propaganda parties. They are only the starting point of a more complex narrative pattern. This makes them even more versatile in terms of communication and potentiates their manipulative possibilities.

Chapter 6

Lies and Truth—and a Final Twist in the Confusion Game

The propagandist will not, especially on the most potent issues, simply let the lie stand as a lie. He will repeat it, but it must not become static, uncool, old news without value. So he continues to work with it. Above all, he strives for one thing: to make the lie "true". To do this, he pretends the lie is true and requires urgent action. And then he acts. He builds real actions on the foundation of the falsehood. Reality is heaped on fiction. Would the party go to all this trouble if there were no truth in it?

It is making the lie "true". The propaganda warrior thus intensifies the "oscillation of lie and truth," intensifies the game of confusion, and dynamizes his story of lies. It persists. It gets new ingredients, remains tellable, and produces news through which the lie are retold, and must be recounted from a journalistic point of view to understand the backstory. All this keeps his story of lies in the media spotlight. Once again, a propaganda strategy mercilessly exploits media mechanisms and harnesses the press to its cause, whether they like it or not. By actively fueling the narrative of lies, the propagandist retains sovereignty over the story's framing and maintains the frame by populating it with content.

Examples abound. In Poland, for instance, things did not end with the conspiracy allegation about Smolensk described in the previous chapter. The official investigation report on the presidential plane crash was taken off the government's website after the PiS election victory. A new commission of inquiry was set up, although its members' qualifications to determine the causes of a plane crash were questionable. Aviation experts who had given their expertise to the first commission of inquiry were interrogated, their private homes searched, and their computers confiscated. Inquiries were made in intelligence circles as to whether there were any findings on Smolensk. However, according to Anne Applebaum, a historian and journalist living in Poland, the commission never found a credible alternative explanation.[1] The PiS party had undertaken considerable efforts and carried out several very visible activities. It expanded its communicative dominance. Above all, Applebaum points out that the PiS party had created a yardstick for loyalty with the Smolensk lie: whoever believed in the Smolensk conspiracy was a good patriot, belonged, and could get posts and support.

Viktor Orbán's Fidesz party has built up one central fabrication in Hungary. George Soros is at the heart of it. According to Orbán's conspiracy allegation, the elderly stock market billionaire—Hungarian, Jewish, living in the United States—favors large-scale immigration. At his universities, he breeds an elite to undermine the nation. Ultimately, this man wants to destroy Hungarian identity in collusion with the European Union, with money and influence, bypassing the will of the voters. He's someone who makes the puppets in Brussels dance. Keyword: repopulation. The whole story of lies is unrestrainedly rooted in anti-Semitic conspiracy allegations as well as anti-elitist and anti-European resentment.

A campaign advisor to Orbán publicly admitted in 2018 to have been part of the team that deliberately built up Soros as public enemy number one. Developing a public enemy was part of the consulting team's strategy to run successful campaigns. An opponent was deliberately sought whom Orbán could vanquish in the name of the Hungarian people. Since the political opposition was too weak, Soros was chosen.[2]

The German business weekly *WirtschaftsWoche* pointed out that Soros has no real influence on immigration policy, either in Hungary or in the EU. He had also never run for office.[3] Soros merely comments on political issues and expresses his opinion. In other words, the political opponent, the competition for Orbán, had to be heavily constructed and invented. The lie was born.

And this lie also had to become "true". To this end, Fidesz denounced the civil society and nongovernmental organizations as stooges of foreign powers and put the screws on them. In the 1990s and the 2000s, Soros's Open Society Foundation enjoyed an excellent reputation in Hungary. However, during Soros's demonization, it was no longer recognized in Hungary; incidentally, the same became true in Russia. Moreover, Orbán targeted the Central European University as an alleged hotbed of anti-Hungarian activity. It, too, was expelled from the country. Along with the story of the invented enemy of the state, Fidesz thus piled real actions, which it exploited for propaganda purposes.

The Orbán advisor declared in an interview, "The perfect opponent is one you hit again and again, and he never hits back."[4] Soros as a "product" had marketed itself. So Orbán expanded his supposed epic struggle against Soros even further, creating new facts, spinning news, and composing new realities that further embellished the frame of the lie. With the "Stop Soros" law, Hungary criminalized refugee helpers who assist migrants in making asylum applications. From a series of public statements by Soros, the propagandists later even built the claim that there was a "Soros Plan." Roughly summarized, this plan was to increase immigration, force the nations of Europe to accept the migrants, and even punish the countries if they violated it. Hungarian EU Commissioner Tibor Navracsics, a member of Orbán's Fidesz, declared there was no evidence of a "Soros Plan."[5] But the propaganda machine was running at full speed. In a national consultation in 2017, Orbán finally called on his compatriots to take a stand on the—nonexistent—"Soros Plan." Millions of people were forced to engage with the lie invented by Orbán. A theatrical discourse in its purest form.

As with the Smolensk lie, the lie of the enemy of the state is made true through great effort and proactive engagement, and the scrutiny of George Soros—friend or foe?—is installed as the fundamental question of the raison d'état.

Making lies dynamic is the practicable part of making lies true because in the process, lies achieve remarkable longevity. The story of the invented enemy of the state has been going on in Hungary since 2012. And it is propagandistically still unfinished. The claim that Obama was not born in the United States and was illegitimately president persisted in the public debate for at least three years, despite all the counterevidence Obama gradually presented. A cheap lie in which every retort was met with a barrage of doubts. In Trump Republican circles, these lies are still considered "truth" to this day (and meanwhile, they are also being spread about the current vice president Kamala Harris).

In Germany, for example, the lie about an alleged dictatorship of opinion has enjoyed great longevity. The persistent reinterpretation generates it in the corresponding meta-frame. For example, if you enter this AfD (Alternative fur Deutschland) buzzword on Twitter, you can find new hits that bring up various current events as alleged evidence. A critical interview with a controversial thinker? Well, look at the question the news presenter asked. He is controlled. They are brainwashing the media—proof of the dictatorship of opinion. And why have an opinion dictatorship? To, as could be read on Twitter in the summer of 2022, "send German citizens into their political, cultural, and financial demise."

The example of opinion dictatorship shows how

critical conspiracy allegations function for propaganda parties. They prepare or make use of a complete interpretative framework. Current individual events are read into these meta-frames and recontextualized. This contextuality is the supposed evidence: I know this is happening because there is something bigger behind it. In this way, a lie can also be made "true."

The strategy of dynamizing a lie by expanding it and making it "true" is also found in Nazi propaganda—in the cruelest, most misanthropic form. As is all too well known, the Nazis built a real empire of hatred and inhumanity on the fictitious claim that there was a Jewish world conspiracy. An elaborate bureaucracy was set up to screen ancestors for Jewish blood. The Nazis manufactured a pseudoscience, among other things, by founding the Munich Institute for Research into the Jewish Question in 1933. Every action was a new opportunity for communication within the frame of the alleged Jewish world conspiracy. Racial doctrine, racial committees, marriage laws, the permeation of school lessons with racial content, the outlawing of Jews in public spaces, pogroms, assaults, racial society, mass murder, and the Holocaust.[6]

The uninhibited Nazi racist obsession that dominated the Nazi state should be a warning to all who think propaganda today is just some sinister PR and marketing magic by a few overpaid spin doctors and political consultants who feed their witchcraft to those obsessed with power. Some are dirty. Russian propaganda is sometimes tantalizingly crude. Other countries are more skillful. All methods and tricks are part and parcel of politics: a bit of media nonsense, and conspiracy talk that only fools fall for. Nothing is more dangerous for liberal democracies than to underestimate contemporary propaganda parties and turn away, relieved when the spook is supposedly over after an election.

But propaganda counts another tool among its instruments of confusion: the truth. Nazi leadership celebrated Hitler and Goebbels for announcing the war, even for their war crimes, and the "final solution to the Jewish question" in their speeches. However, the general public considered those speeches to be nothing but groundless provocation. Hannah Arendt summarized this as follows:

> "The environment accuses them of demagogy just when they openly state what they mean. Of course, Bolshevists and Nazis alike have exploited in many ways this inability of the nontotalitarian world to believe them."[7]

Trump's wall propaganda is one recent prominent example of this inability of the nontotalitarian world. His announcement of a wall on the border with Mexico initially provoked disbelief and amusement among many. In liberal circles in the US, the move was perceived as an excessive provocation, not as a realistic policy option in the fight against illegal immigration. Trump's supporters understood this message differently—and better. What is crucial for the propagandistic venom is that these "honest" moments of the leaders leave people pondering. Every time they make another statement, people wonder how the latest slogan, advance, and insult will be understood. They have to consider that the statement could be true. In terms of communication strategy, this maximizes uncertainty through the well-dosed interplay of lies and truth. It's the final turn of the screw of the confusion game meant to destroy the individual's sense of reality. "Maybe it is, maybe it isn't. How was that meant now? And have I perhaps been looking at it the wrong way all along? Does the fault lie with me?" This phenomenon is now known as gaslighting, a term that has become well-established in the propaganda debate. Initially, it was used in science to refer to psychological violence in interpersonal relationships. Those who gaslight deny the victim's reality, facts, and perceptions repeatedly or question them incessantly until the victim's self-doubt becomes so great that their sense of reality is permanently derailed. And this is what propaganda tries to achieve with its confusing game of lies and truth. The game of confusion causes not only the population but also the media to puzzle over facts and lies—and so a single tweet by Trump filled entire broadcasts of the US news channels, again and again. The propaganda party ceaselessly tries to create chaos of opinion. For amid the confusion, the firm voice of its leader, together with clear and straightforward solutions within an extensive framework (of meta-frames), is particularly effective in reaching people and attracting them, as they want to be delivered from uncertainty and disorientation. The confusion ensures that the question of lies or truth becomes irrelevant in the minds of the masses.

Propaganda parties transform factual questions into emotionally charged issues of faith. They draw political competitors and observers onto their playing field, where they have the advantage of competence and planning. And through their constant stream of propaganda, they have long prepared people for this playing field. On a massive scale, they have formed content and contexts so that followers see, interpret, and classify all future information through propaganda. Acting aggressively on this playing field is what the propaganda parties believe will bring them the most benefit on their way to power for power's sake.

Chapter 7

Continuous Attack: The Battle for Norms, Facts, and a Worldview

As the previous chapters have shown, propaganda uses various communication tools to spread its message as intensely and effectively as possible. Breaking communication norms serves to underpin the political idea of the propaganda party and generate credibility. Conspiracy allegations create large interpretive frames that make this idea narratable and supposedly provable. By lying and confusing lies and truth, the propaganda pushes voters onto its favored arena, the world of belief, where people become particularly seducible. But this does not happen without hurdles and democratic opposition, which a propaganda party has to overcome.

In the eyes of propagandists, democratic institutions cannot be neutral, honest, credible, or independent. After all, they are part of the existing system—and a party that positions itself outside the system must treat parts of the system as it treats the system as a whole: as enemies. Besides the government, the institutions targeted by the propaganda warriors include parliament, the courts, (public) broadcasters, and academia, which use evidence- or research-based approaches to understanding reality.

It's hardly a surprise that we can discern historical parallels here as well. Goebbels, for example, invented the fairy tale of a Jewish "lying press," and he openly recounted how the Nazis acted against them: "They lie! They lie! With this battle cry, we countered the Jewish cannonade of filth."[1]

This rallying cry seems to echo in the present. Let us think back to Trump's first press conference as president of the United States in January 2017, when he hurled the infamous phrase "You are fake news!" at a CNN reporter in attendance. Goebbels positioned the press as the antithesis of the people's will with the additional help of an excellent reflex: he declared it had "become the scourge of the people."[2] Trump repeatedly called the *New York Times* and CNN "enemies of the American people."[3] Propaganda politicians worldwide seized on this choice of words, this outsized interpretive framework, and attacked the media, especially the public broadcasters.

Like Hitler, Goebbels also made extensive fun of scientists and intellectuals. Today, climate researchers and health experts are targets of a propaganda-fueled mélange of trolls, conspiracy mongers, and angry citizens. Similarly, when a court ruling complicated the process of Brexit, the tabloid *Daily Mail* in England ran the headline "Enemies of the people."[4] At the end of the 1920s, Goebbels called parliament "a stinking dung heap"[5] that needed to be mucked out. He left no doubt by whom: "We come as enemies! As the wolf breaks into the flock of sheep, so we come."[6] The Nazis went to the Reichstag to "enter democracy's arsenal and stock up on its weapons":

> "We become Reichstag deputies to cripple the Weimar spirit with its assistance. If democracy is so stupid as to give us expense accounts and parliamentary allowances for this disservice, that is its affair."[7]

Parliament, as the home of pluralism, is to propagandists and their satellite organizations a particularly offensive symbol of liberal democracy allegedly acting against the interests of the people. This sentiment was echoed in the storming of the Reichstag in Berlin in August 2020. And in the storming of the Capitol on January 6, 2021, encouraged by a sitting president. Later, Trump tweeted, "I know your pain. I know you're hurt. We had an election that was stolen from us. It was a landslide election, and everyone knows it, especially the other side."[8] Five people died during the storming of the Capitol. Social media turned off Trump's channels only when faced with an attempted coup and the foreshadowing of civil war.

The public debate focuses a great deal on the structural imbalance of institutions. By attacking institutions, propaganda is attacking the organizational backbone of democracy, as the examples illustrate. However, it is worthwhile to look at another aspect for communicative understanding. The structural function of institu-

tions is one thing, and the actions of their representatives and the performance of their duties are others.
Parliamentarians and judges set norms. Journalists and
scientists collect facts and interpret our world.

Norm-makers, fact-gatherers, world-interpreters—
propagandist ideology must fight them all. There are
several reasons for this:

1. It is notably the norm-makers, fact-gatherers, and
   world-interpreters who can bring down propaganda's edifice of lies and expose their deception.
2. If the electorate sees people and sources as legiti-
   mate, they will be much less receptive to propagandist messages.
3. If norm-makers, fact-gatherers, and world-interpreters get to determine the socially accepted arena
   of debate by providing basic information, this will
   severely restrict propaganda's sphere of action.
4. Propaganda parties do not want to be seen chasing
   the issues and arguments of their self-chosen enemies since, otherwise, they cannot put their basic
   notion of being outside the mainstream into prac-
   tice and determine the discourse.

Given these scenarios, propaganda cannot be passive.
And in their view, being proactive includes, crucially,
pursuing aggressive personal attacks. Anything is acceptable that discredits norm builders, fact gatherers,
and world interpreters, including systematic online attacks on critical journalists, which can last for years.[9]

Scientists are exposed to cyberbullying, threats of violence, and hatred. Anthony Fauci and the German virologist Christian Drosten are just two recent examples of this.

Anyone who raises their voice has automatically entered the arena. Anyone whose statements do not suit the propaganda is targeted, with the explicit intention of intimidating and silencing them. The propaganda warriors promote violence and cyberbullying, and even condone political murders. Various public figures have had to seek police protection, at least temporarily, in the face of such threats.

"We are pure. The others are evil. None of them does anything without an ulterior motive. Everyone is potentially part of a secret system." Such is the paranoid view of humanity that propagandists espouse every day. It is a view that distrusts the system's mostly functional checks and balances, and discounts any complexity introduced by divergent political interests, rival personal ambitions, or coincidences and improbable events. In this worldview, there are no respectable politicians, honest journalists, impartial judges, or trustworthy scientists outside their ranks. There is only us and them. There is no individuality, critical thinking, or dissent within the democratic system. Many supporters of propaganda parties adhere to this gloomy and destructive view of humanity.

Should the norm-makers, fact-gatherers, and world-interpreters ever slip up with an actual transgression, they instantly become sitting ducks for propaganda. Because for propaganda to succeed, outrage must be kept at a fever pitch, and anger has to be continuously fueled. The easier the transgression can be woven into one's interpretive frames and narratives, the better. A blunder in a newscast or a scientist misquoting a fact instantly provides full "proof" that the "lying press" is deliberately deceptive, that government is a joke, and that the courts are judging against the will of the people.

To get ahead of the norm-makers, fact-gatherers, and world-interpreters, propaganda warriors must keep the speed of their communication very high to fan the breathlessness of a polarized society. Unfortunately, political processes, scientifically sound research, and thorough investigative analysis take time. On the Web, on the other hand, propaganda promotes opinion forming in real time by making topics minimally plausible and maximally palpable through large interpretive meta-frames.

If they can, propaganda politicians use state media, like the way Putin does in Russia, Erdoğan in Turkey, or Orbán in Hungary. Others use their own or "alternative" media. But even more critical are, and will remain, the independent media because they allow even more friction to be generated. Propagandists work intensively off the reaction of their enemies to intensify and prolong the conflict they have created. The right-wing platform Breitbart News had perfected this approach under Steve Bannon. Journalist Michael Wolff identifies a corresponding paradigm shift in contemporary politics: "The new politics was not about the art of compromise, but the art of conflict."[10]

Through confrontation and provocation, propagandists activate media mechanisms by deliberately appealing to emotional news values such as sensationalism, surprise, negativity, or personalization. Such news values strongly influence whether the media pick up a news item. More factual aspects—which should likewise determine the news value of an item—play, at best, a subordinate role.

A straightforward and effective propaganda tool is that of the public dilemma. If a propaganda politician were invited on a talk show, he would complain about how unfairly he was treated there. But if he were not invited, "they" wanted to silence him. The propaganda politician will take both these versions to the public, thus forcing the media to pick up the talking point, as this is the only way they can report on it in a meaningful way. The cat-and-mouse game also works for conspiracy allegations. If journalists criticize such claims as false or fabricated, they are, according to propaganda, acting against the people's will. They are confronted with a torrent of hostilities and alleged evidence, and are thus forced to remain silent or continue engaging on the propaganda warriors' turf. If they do not address conspiracy allegations, this proves the journalists are in cahoots with the evil forces. The examples show that such dilemmas can be constructed almost endlessly with little effort.

Everything is designed to discredit and defame the norm makers, fact gatherers, and world interpreters for maximum effect. The content is highly interchangeable. Propaganda more often plays and expands content that captures the imagination. Any content that doesn't fit the bill is replaced. Content is nothing but ammunition. Hannah Arendt already noted such an "emptying of all content"[11] for the Nazi state. This emptiness and arbitrariness, as well as their flexibility regarding issues and topics, seems to be a constant of propaganda parties. Everything serves the primary goal of reaching the masses on an emotional level and making them compliant. The bait must be attractive to the fish, not the fisher.

Chapter 8
Group Behavior on Social Media

Media presence and effectiveness play a unique role for propagandists. President Trump seemed obsessed with the media's perception of him. It was widely reported that he often spent hours watching coverage of himself on television. He was not always satisfied with what he saw. And that made it all the more critical for him to reach his supporters directly. In 2020, as acting president, he sent out 12,239 tweets, i. e., 36 tweets and retweets per day. That was his personal Twitter record. In 2019, he managed "only" 7,800 tweets, an average of 21 tweets and retweets daily.[1] Still, he was reaching a large audience. At the beginning of 2020, he had sixty-seven million followers on Twitter, more than Angela Merkel, Boris Johnson, Emmanuel Macron, and the Pope combined.[2] In France, Marine Le Pen has long been considered a "social media queen."[3] The Austrian Freedom Party (FPÖ) has invested significant resources in its media offerings. FPÖ-TV, for example, is the model for Germany's AfD-TV. Former FPÖ officials also run the website unzensuriert.at ("uncensored").

In Germany, the AfD has for years ranked far above all other political parties in social media activity. It is particularly present on Facebook. In the 2021 German federal election campaign, party leader Weidel's social media videos were viewed 4.9 million times in just two and a half months. All other top candidates achieved only a fraction of that. Armin Laschet, the Christian Democratic Union candidate for chancellor, had 320,000 views. Weidel was also number one in interaction, sharing, and commenting on posts.[4] This is no coincidence. The AfD put enormous resources into social media and communication and took advice from Harris Media, the social media agency that had previously worked with Trump. The AfD considers everyone in its ranks to be a "social media soldier" in the information war, as one AfD politician put it.[5]

The reasons for this focus on social media have already been discussed. The advantages for these parties include directly communicating and bonding with the electorate, creating one's own media spaces, bypassing traditional media, getting complete control over the message, setting one's issues, and agenda surfing, i.e., jumping on viral topics on the Internet for their positioning and recruitment of followers.

The focus here shall be on another compelling aspect: group psychological effects in social media. These effects contribute to the rise of hate speech we've been observing for years, and precisely these effects are fueled and driven by propaganda parties and their sympathizers on the Web. Research on group psychology has its origins in the late nineteenth century. In 1895, the physician and ethnologist Gustave Le Bon published his book *The Crowd* and has since been regarded as the founder of modern group psychology. His work is still cited today. Le Bon's subject of study was French politics since the Revolution of 1789. The Nazis were strongly influenced by Le Bon and contemporary writings that drew on his psychology of the masses. And even today, we have to consider his insights when we think of modern propaganda strategies.

According to Le Bon, a group can become an organized crowd whose feelings and thoughts converge under certain circumstances. A communal spirit is formed, a single indeterminate being. "Whoever be the individuals that compose it, however like or unlike be their mode of life, their occupations, their character, or their intelligence."[6]

Le Bon believed that what happens in these groups is transference. Every feeling and every action can be influenced and transferred, so much so that "an individual readily sacrifices his personal interest to the collective interest."[7] He is no longer himself, almost hypnotized. The individual's concept of the impossible fades in the group.

The Nazis' large-scale events have to be seen against this background. Masses had to come together physically so transmission would be possible and people could align themselves with the führer. All propaganda was aimed at conquering the masses, Goebbels wrote. Large-scale staged marches were the central instrument of Nazi propaganda to produce group behavior. The numerous Nazi events, some involving more than a million people, in their absurd opulence and overdriven imagery, have burned themselves into the collective memory.

Such marches—apart from much smaller demonstrations—have practically disappeared. "We are many" is a reference to mass that can often be read on social media. It is something between a call to battle, a self-acclamation, and an attempt to intimidate dissenters. In this book, I argue that social media has taken over the meaning and purpose of group events. The case of German politician Renate Künast shows this very impressively. The Green Party leader became the target of crude insults and slander on the Internet. In response, she went to the homes of some people who had insulted her online. She was greeted with surprise and politeness and was able to have reasonable conversations with them. A collective group behavior had emerged toward her on the Web, but it vanished in real life. People, confronted individually, dealt with Künast quite differently.

Social media offers much better and more far-reaching possibilities for today's propaganda than simple group events. The platforms are available seven days a week, twenty-four hours a day. They require less effort, have a greater reach, and can be used to measure each message's impact. Moreover, each statement can be broadcast to a specific target group as determined by usage data called "microtargeting." In addition, the constant availability of information makes it possible to spread propaganda permanently, thus ratcheting up the confirmation bias almost ad infinitum, i. e., people's unconscious preference for information and interpretations that confirm their convictions.

Moreover, social media enables what John Oddo,

an American linguist and communications scholar, has called "horizontal propaganda,"[8] which complements and extends "classic" vertical propaganda from above or from the top of the propaganda party. In horizontal propaganda, the impulse is transported horizontally at the right time via relevant groups, advocacy organizations, sympathizers, trolls, and bots through sharing and commenting. The propagandist only has to set the impulses. Dissemination and persuasion are done by others, who are thereby bonded even more strongly to the propaganda party. The propaganda party is confirmed as the only authentic voice of the people since its propaganda is transported and authenticated by the people themselves—snowball propaganda.

We must acknowledge that social media is shaped by group psychology. Corresponding effects are prevalent there, and group behavior can be deliberately generated. Individuals seem to feel anonymous on the Web, as if they are part of a mass. Social media is seen as a lawless space where nothing will happen if you go too far.

According to Le Bon, individuals in a crowd feel a sense of invincible power. At the same time, anonymity breeds irresponsibility. An individual's intuitive sense of responsibility often disappears completely. This leads to a special kind of behavior:

> "Isolated, he may be a cultivated individual; in a crowd, he is a barbarian—that is, a creature acting by instinct. He possesses the spontaneity, the violence, the ferocity, and also the enthusiasm and heroism of primitive beings."[9]

The crowd adds "impulsiveness, irritability, incapacity to reason, the absence of judgment and the critical spirit, the exaggeration of the sentiments."[10] The crowd is intolerant.

"An individual may accept contradiction and discussion; a crowd will never do so. At public meetings, the slightest contradiction on the part of an orator is immediately received with howls of fury and violent invective, soon followed by blows and expulsion should the orator stick to his point. Without the restraining presence of the representatives of authority, the contradictor, indeed, would often be done to death."[11] In 1960, philosopher and Nobel laureate in literature Elias Canetti coined the term "baiting crowd" in *Crowds and Power*.[12] It is startling how much these descriptions made long ago fit today's social media world. We have often seen discussions of social media's brutalization, a world out of control, overflowing verbal aggression, slander, hate speech, murder fantasies and threats, and the inability and unwillingness to engage in dialogue. Everyone is shouting down everyone else on the Web. The irritable society is most evident there. This unbridled disinhibition has often been attributed to technologically generated filter bubbles—and to echo chambers created by the networking of like-minded people. The thesis is that all this is due to group behavior that can be triggered on the Web—and is being triggered deliberately by propagandists. As masters of manipulation, they can shape masses on the Internet. Their guiding principle seems to be to "fuel group behavior."

This interpretation is also borne out by contemporary research. Business psychologist Thomas Brudermann has researched group psychological dynamics. According to this research, several factors influence whether the information is transmitted in a mass-psychological way. Brudermann speaks of "contagion." For him, the two most important factors are, on the one hand, the number and influence of the initial agents, i. e., actors who deliberately bring information into the world at the earliest stage. The other is the individual stimulus threshold. "It determines whether and how easily a person is infected with a psychological pathogen, for example, a particular political attitude [. . .] by other people."[13] Minimal shifts in the average stimulus thresholds are decisive for whether a message catches on or not.

This leads us directly to the critical realization that propagandists have three primary goals in social media: They want to increase the number of participants in the process in general. They additionally seek to increase the number of initial agents with influence (by number of followers and interactions). And they want to lower the individual irritation threshold. They try to generate great emotion and recurring escalation of particular topics, such as migration, to achieve these goals. In addition, they work to intensify the horizontal propaganda mentioned above, primarily through conspiracy allegations, meta-frames, and the muddling of lies and truth.

Social media is the perfect tool for emotional contagion—for good and for ill. Finnish investigative journalist and renowned analyst of the information wars Jessikka Aro warns that in the hands of propagandists, social media can become "psychological weapons of mass destruction."[14] Social networks have negated their fundamental responsibility for this for a very long time. In 2011, for example, Google employee Guillaume Chaslot pointed out internally that YouTube's algorithm was built to offer more and more of the same content. This could lead to untrue content being massively pushed by the algorithm. He suggested how Google could counteract this and keep content diverse, but his bosses pushed the issue aside.[15] Facebook CEO Mark Zuckerberg has argued for years that freedom of speech and expression prevail on his platform. And he has granted politicians more and more of this "freedom"—the freedom without hindrance to spread lies, agitation, and calls for violence, some of which have ended in deadly attacks. What an abuse of the notion of freedom of expression. What a cheap PR charade.

Part of this freedom was, of course, to run million-dollar ad campaigns on Facebook. The algorithm that fueled and massively spread sensationalism and traffic was not up for debate. Only when Trump spread the "stolen election" lie on election night in November 2021 did Facebook resort to an emergency change to the newsfeed algorithm. In other words, such a change had always been possible. "News Ecosystem Quality," as Facebook calls it, was now given a higher weighting, i.e., verifiable quality media were given more attention and prominence by the algorithm. It turns out that Facebook could favor journalistic trustworthiness and reliable sources. In their book *Inside Facebook*, *New York Times* journalists Sheera Frenkel and Cecilia Kang wrote, "For five days after the vote, Facebook seemed a calmer, less divisive place."[16]

The negative, inflammatory, reality-defying group psychological effect of propaganda, hate, and misinformation could be permanently mitigated and contained by social media operators. However, Facebook found that the "nicer" newsfeed generated fewer views and shorter dwell times. This wasn't good for business. Greed and self-importance made Zuckerberg an enabler of dictators and those who aspire to be.

Of course, these group psychological effects have not escaped the attention of Facebook and other social networks. For example, Facebook conducted a clandestine experiment back in 2012. Some users were shown happy content; others, sad. It turned out that negative posts made users react with negative statements, while positive content led to users expressing themselves more positively. In 2014, Facebook published a research report and then made the experiment public. In it, Facebook employees wrote:

"Emotional states can be transferred to others via emotional contagion, leading people to experience the same emotions without their awareness"[17]

Social media creators know about their platforms' group psychological potential. Propaganda parties use them.

According to Le Bon, the masses only know extreme feelings. For this reason, affection for a leader quickly turns into worship, "worship of a being supposed superior, fear of the power with which the being is credited, blind submission to its commands, inability to discuss its dogmas, the desire to spread them, and a tendency to consider as enemies all by whom they are not accepted."[18]

This religious motif, to the point of servility, is known to have played a central role in Hitler's regime. Goebbels deliberately orchestrated it. Today, supporters celebrate propaganda politicians like Orbán and Erdoğan as saviors. Donald Trump, again, has exhausted the arsenal of propaganda like no other. We often hear about Trump's "fan base." The term "fan," on closer inspection, is pretty accurate. Many of Trump's supporters have built a fanatical emotional attachment to him. The storming of the Capitol after just a few vague sentences from him is perhaps the best and, at the same time, most sinister evidence of this. During his speech shortly before, Trump and his fans had assured each other of their "love." His fans admire him, partly regard him as a "savior," forgive him, and, crucially, believe him. Trump has turned the Republican party into a kind of cult, according to some, even within the party.[19] Le Bon outlined, almost like a manual, how a leader can establish worship and allegiance in his speeches to the masses. The speaker should "never appeal to the rationality" of the crowd. The speaker must give the impression of sharing people's feelings before deliberately manipulating them. The speaker must use explicit expressions, simple language, and strong images because only intense feelings activate the crowd. The crowd's logic is characterized by the superficial linking of similar things and the hasty generalization of individual cases, and a leader must cater to that.[20] This is how propaganda politicians talk about the Jews, the Muslims, and the "rapists" from Latin America. They ingratiate themselves as the true voice of the people with such audacity that only collectivist obliviousness can explain why people should fall for this pandering for their favor, far removed from any consideration of content. The propaganda politicians' forceful expressions and norm-breaking language were already dealt with earlier. They talk the talk of the people because their fundamental objective—power for power's sake—demands it.

According to Le Bon, the leader's task is to inspire belief and to be a fixed point of reference for the crowd. To do this, the leader must bring an idea to the crowd, which takes a great deal of time and effort. "When by various processes an idea has ended by penetrating the minds of crowds, it possesses an irresistible power."[21] At this point, the political idea, whose critical role was already explained in the second chapter, also acquires psychological relevance. Embodied by the leader, it becomes the largest possible and longest-lasting framework that can direct masses and promote desired behavior.

Le Bon also examined the relationship crowds have with lies and truths. Crowds cannot be influenced by logic, he concluded. Miraculous and legendary aspects most effectively capture them. The unreal always takes precedence over the real. Crowds must be excessively credulous, and nothing seems improbable to them. This is how the most improbable legends and reports emerge.[22] Lie or truth—it does not matter to the crowd. It ignores unpleasant facts, while it turns without hesitation to lies that have a seductive effect. Le Bon concludes that one can easily control the masses if one knows how to deceive them and that one has already lost if one tries to enlighten them.[23]

In connection with this gullibility of the masses, Le Bon picked up on conspiracy allegations of his time and already described at the end of the nineteenth century how receptive crowds could be to conspiracy allegations. And so psychology reveals why propaganda politicians have a special relationship with lies and truth: The masses do not seek the truth. They seek validation.

Chapter 9
Diffusion Chambers, Spillover, and Staircase Arguments

The previous chapters presented strategies such as horizontal propagation, group psychological contagion, or seduction utilizing connecting thoughts and feelings. The question is how do these strategies work on a tactical and practical level? How are they implemented? This chapter will focus on three patterns propagandists often use: diffusion chambers, spillover, and staircase arguments.

One issue that has been getting a lot of attention in the media and politics is the idea of so-called echo chambers on the Web. This phenomenon—together with filter bubbles created by algorithms—contributes to the polarization of society. The notion of echo chambers suggests that like-minded people withdraw into their networks and form virtually closed spaces in which they reinforce and sometimes radicalize each other's views and attitudes. But this explanation does not go far enough. It leaves room for the misconception that there are no overarching interests at play but only the coincidental interplay of two particular interests: the desire of a group to be among like-minded people and the commercial interest of platform operators like Meta to activate profitable user behavior through recommendations. What is underestimated or even overlooked is how much the echo chambers can be exploited for propaganda purposes. And how they are exploited daily.

Echo chambers are only supposedly closed to the outside: in at least two situations, they are semi- or selectively permeable. First of all, to new members. Experience has shown that echo chambers usually grow and rarely shrink. So it must be possible for new members to join the echo chamber by liking, sharing, and commenting. The chamber is thus permeable to incoming sympathizers. New members may already share the core beliefs that prevail in the echo chamber. They may have learned about this space for like-minded people only recently. Delayed entry occurs.

Much more important, however, is the second case of semipermeability. Here, the echo chamber deliberately plays out content across its borders. It is intended to reach people who have not previously been part of the echo chamber but may have issue-specific, aligned opinions and attitudes. In Germany, AfD-aligned circles, for example, make intensive efforts to reach out to the conservative circles of the mainstream conservative CDU and the national-liberal circles within the more libertarian FDP. It could be about an enemy or a theme of outrage that, in principle, appeals to several circles. Such an approach may be described as a spillover tactic. The propagandistic spark is supposed to jump over to people who are within reach of one's views and attitudes. Corresponding analyses show how particular messages broadcast outside the echo chamber create a targeted response. Echo chambers are, therefore, really predominantly diffusion chambers. Propaganda uses these secure, semipermeable havens of crowd psychology to its advantage.

Spillover tactics also target the traditional media. They are encouraged, if not driven, to report on something. Individual journalists are tagged. Their name and account are linked to the content so they are aware of the issue. They are also specifically addressed and asked not to remain silent about this—alleged—scandal. The benefit is obvious: letting a topic spill over from a chamber into the mainstream media ennobles it, increases its credibility, and maximizes its reach. A perfect amplifier.

Very pointed, provocative statements are among the most blatant examples. A frequently cited example in this context is a tweet by German politician Marcus Pretzell, then leader of the AfD in North Rhine-Westphalia. "They are Merkel's dead," he posted a few minutes after the murderous terrorist attack on Berlin's Breitscheidplatz on Christmas 2016 by a Tunisian asylum seeker named Anis Amri. Pretzell dominated parts of the discussions on the Web and more than a few headlines in the mainstream media with this tweet. Pretzell explained that he used social media to "trigger journalists."[1] This is how spillover works. Again, this maneuver is part of the propagandist's agenda. And again: Constant dripping wears away the stone. The same groove is struck time and again.

But there are also more ambitious spillover maneuvers. From my time as head of communications at German public broadcaster ARD, I can cite the "Imperial Flag" story. Early October 2020, the Web was suddenly in an uproar on the Saturday morning of a long holiday weekend. A short video triggered it. It showed two men taking a flag of the pre-1918 German empire out of the trunk of their car. They were ostensibly about to join a demonstration against the government's coronavirus policy organized by the "Querdenker" (lateral thinkers) movement in Cologne. The film was made by a passerby who asked the men whether they had to bring that thing to the protest. That is all. This brief interaction was turned into a story in the right-wing bubble, alleging that the two men were provocateurs, employees of our affiliate station WDR, out to discredit the event. If no one at the demo was carrying a Reich flag, WDR would simply have to generate the "right" images for themselves. Two portrait photos from WDR websites were cited as evidence to identify the two "perpetrators."

Later analyses showed how members of the diffusion chamber wanted to trigger a shitstorm and simulate great outrage through coordinated sharing and commenting. Again, bots may have played a supporting role. In a short time, algorithms jumped at the high traffic because the topic seemed to measurably generate the right amount of conversation and quantitatively relevant exchange, both of which have become essential social media currencies. Consequently, the algorithm automatically boosted the original post by making it accessible to wider circles and giving it preferential exposure.

Several journalists were alerted to the flag allegation. Less than an hour after it was first published on the Internet, I was contacted by an annoyed journalist who said he was constantly being tagged and had to investigate the matter because the accusation warranted reporting. He told me he would need a statement or clarification before the editorial deadline in the next two hours. Now, you try to check whether a single person in a video may be affiliated with your company in even the broadest sense. And then try doing that within two hours on a weekend in an organization with thousands of permanent staff, many more freelancers, and numerous production companies.

Meanwhile, the diffusion chamber was churning to create spillover. It cited alleged evidence, and further suspicions—the mass psychological propaganda machine on the Web was working to generate live opinions. And a major newspaper was already preparing a piece on the affair. The accusations were soon refuted, which was in turn doubted and questioned with alleged counterevidence. Then, the following day, one of the two men in the video publicly identified himself as a "patriot" who had taken part in the demonstration of his own free will, out of his conviction, and without any connection to our organization.

The alleged connection to our affiliate station had thus been freely invented, presumably hoping it would do some damage. This tactic has long been called "rotten herring" in propaganda literature; something of the stink of suspicion will remain. The news, after all, is always bigger than the correction.

Especially in core debates, propaganda supports and orchestrates the spillover tactic through very specific and manipulative rhetoric. This rhetoric is designed to make it as easy as possible for doubters to agree. Followers are also given persuasive language to spread. This propaganda rhetoric will be referred to here as staircase arguments. These lead step-by-step to the position of the propaganda party.

This technique can be seen as a further development of the 60/40 method, which Goebbels is supposed to have invented. In it, 60 percent of a narrative has to be factual to gain the readers' trust. An added 40 percent contains the intended misinformation, which gives the item its propagandistic value.

Staircase arguments are no longer about press coverage and facts. They are about directly reaching people on the Web through value judgments. The first step involves a statement many agree with, ideally even a majority. With this, the propagandists throw out an anchor of acceptability. They claim socially widely accepted positions for themselves, but these merely serve as an acceptable derivative of a different position. The actual position then appears more "middle-of-the-road" and acceptable than it would be on its own. Stirrup holder arguments are used here, serving as camouflage to infiltrate the broader public. The second and third steps of the staircase must also reach and be comprehensible to a broad target group; they must get beyond the hard-core and the second, softer circle of sympathizers of the propaganda party. Only at the end of the staircase argumentation do the party's positions come into play. They are supposed to appear like sensible conclusions from a series of previously agreed-upon theses. The actual position is thus not at the center but is built up as the culmination of a sham logical chain, which projects inevitability.

Up to this point, the propaganda has ensured that the recipient has repeatedly confirmed the more general statements. Yes, yes, yes—the person is thereby taken in and psychologically aligned. The political distance appears much smaller.

Ultimately, it becomes much easier to say yes to the final radical conclusion.

Staircase arguments serve as a propagandistic plausibility machine. Let's stay with public service broadcasters. These are a feature in most European countries as well as some other countries, where mandatory license fees fund one or more public broadcasters that are independent but are legally obliged to supply balanced and nonpartisan news. American readers may imagine this in the US as the government mandating and enforcing an annual contribution to PBS and NPR from every taxpaying citizen.

In Europe, these broadcasters are commonly confronted with the following argumentative pattern: On the first step of the staircase, propaganda formulates the subsequent thesis: "Public service broadcasting is too expensive."

The statement chosen here is one that many people can agree with in principle. A message that almost seems to be common sense and can be experienced individually. After all, most people in many European countries are legally obliged to pay a broadcasting fee. Step two is the statement "Public broadcasting is too big." Many people will also spontaneously agree with this thesis, even if it will no longer be quite so close to their personal experience.

On the third step, the thesis becomes "By the way, public service broadcasting is also one-sided in its reporting." Naturally, approval of this will decline. But this statement does have its supporters in conservative and libertarian circles.

The fourth step is to claim "Public service broadcasting urgently needs to be reformed." The first conclusion from the previous theses is so general that sympathizers of the first three staircase arguments can largely agree. Thus, the propagandist has produced an agreement with some more general views four times. Four times recipients have inwardly said yes.

After the field has been prepared in content and psychology, the propagandistic message slowly begins to take hold on step five: "Public service broadcasting must be drastically reduced."

And right after that, on level six, we get to the crux of the matter: "Actually, it should be abolished. But we don't want to go there—we want it to be reduced to a basic broadcasting service."

In Germany, this is the current demand of the AfD. It has softened its quite radical position of abolition. Because that demand made it stand alone and isolated, finally, the party had to acknowledge that the demand was not enforceable.

Above all, it was not propagandistically connectable in the sense of spillover tactics. However, the AfD can agree with parts of the libertarian FDP, the conservative CDU, and its sister party CSU about a minimized broadcasting system. The smaller demand has greater appeal and, thus, more propagandistic utility. And once the step has been taken, it is not far to the actual goal of abolition. The real intention—to silence independent observers and critics of propaganda, and to delegitimize representatives of an open society and spaces of social dialogue—remain hidden.

Staircase arguments run through the entire propaganda rhetoric of such parties. Let's take Russia as an example: since 2013, positive remarks about homosexuals in the presence of children became punishable. Moreover, Putin likes to mock "Gayropa" and dubs the democracies of Europe "homocracies."[2] His basic staircase argument is more subtly constructed:

Level 1: We have our own Russian identity.
Level 2: In this, traditional values are important to us.
Level 3: For example, the traditional family value of husband and wife.
Level 4: That is quite normal. Homosexuality is abnormal.
Level 5: The West wants to push the issue of homosexuality on us.
Level 6: We reject this cultural imperialism of the West.

Level 7: The West should stop trying to indoctrinate
         Russian children.

Only at level five does the real propaganda message be-
gin, turning arch-reactionary legislation into an attack
by the West against which Russia must defend itself.

Whether diffusion chambers, spillover tactics, or
staircase argumentation, using all these techniques in
the long term requires a lot of communicative "fodder"
and massive use of resources. It also requires constant
escalation because the initiative must be maintained,
and the masses must be kept in an emotional state of
emergency. Anger and hatred toward the opponents
must be stirred up, and euphoria and commitment to
the common cause must be maintained. Over time, the
stimulus must be ratcheted to capture the attention of
the masses over and over. As Hannah Arendt had already stated after the Nazi era, "a political goal that
would constitute the end of the movement simply does
not exist."[3] SS leader Heinrich Himmler had summed
up the perversion of fascistic self-exaggeration in a
single sentence: natural selection knows no standstill.[4]
Readers may take this thought to its logical conclusion.
Once again, let's note that things that are little known
nor understood today were already openly on the ta-
ble only a few decades earlier. In any case, it is due to
the constant need for escalation that most propaganda politicians become increasingly shrill in their statements and actions as the years go by. Trump no longer
centrally advertises with the famous "Make America
Great Again" but with "Save America," which implies

an apparent increase in the doomsday scenario. He publicly called the incumbent president an "enemy of the state" and spoke of "purges" needed in Washington.[5] This urge and compulsion to outdo themselves makes propaganda politicians more and more dangerous over time because they put themselves under pressure to follow words with actions to maintain their credibility with their supporters.

With diffusion chambers, spillover tactics, and staircase arguments, I presented three techniques in this chapter to demonstrate, on a practical level, how propaganda can be generated and implemented in such a way that it appeals to more and more people—distribution and persuasion in one. This is how propaganda creates waves that roll through the Internet, the media, and the social discourse again and again. The high seas of discord.

Chapter 10
The Poisoned Heart of Democracy

Never has the world—especially the media—been so susceptible to propaganda as it is today. We are witnessing a complete militarization of the communications space. Yet the poison of propaganda is only used superficially against political opponents. Deep down, it is directed against the heart of democracy: societal dialogue.

Liberal democracies always risk exposing themselves to infiltration through the vulnerability and openness of their basic understanding of society. This is both a moral strength and a potential weakness. Propaganda parties have almost perfected consistently poking at the vulnerabilities of the system. The communicative master plan of propaganda politicians serves the overriding goal of making political and social dialogue impossible. It does so not only in its strategies and techniques but, above all, in the sum of its parts. It must willfully destroy dialogue. The public debate, as well as opinion forming—supplied by recognized and competent norm makers, fact gatherers, and world interpreters—runs counter to the propaganda parties' quests to gain and retain power.

Thus, the propaganda warriors operate all the levers that shatter the world of facts and make the search for lies and truth irrelevant. When even basic facts cannot be agreed upon, democratic discourse becomes paralyzed. Society is robbed of its bearings, compass, and basic alignment. In addition, propaganda parties constantly create pressure to decide—are you with them or with us? The Nazis had already created a post-factual world, which they perverted as a totalitarian system in the Second World War—until their downfall.

"There's no talking to him anymore." Propagandists celebrate this phrase as the fruit of their labor. The collapse of political, social, and private-political dialogue is precisely what they want, for this is the heart chamber of liberal democracy, where compromises are born. Compromises that integrate perspectives are the essence of liberal democracy. A democracy that is no longer capable of forging compromises falters. It becomes weak, produces no results, and makes no progress on socially contentious issues. The problems build, and with them, the tensions. Those who stifle social dialogue slowly but surely suffocate open democracy. It loses its vital ability to function. There is less and less compromise and progress pumping through its veins. Problems get jammed, piled up, and accumulated. Propagandists cite this as proof of democracy's failure. The vicious cycle is established. The call for other leaders and approaches grows louder and louder; the propagandists have democracy by the short and curlies. Their hour has come. If they are already in power, this serves to maintain or expand their power.

Propaganda works with misinformation to create total confusion and, fundamentally, to deform social dialogue beyond recognition. So when there is talk of an "erosion" of social dialogue in our polarized society, this observation is euphemistically blurred. Erosion sounds God-given—as if it were an unintended by-product of many influences that no one could have foreseen. The term naively obscures how controlled, deliberate, and driven this "erosion" is. Those who do not see through the propaganda master plan remain defenseless. Those who underestimate the highly negative energy of the propaganda master plan have already lost. You may feel relieved when Trump is voted out of office, the AfD loses votes, and the FPÖ becomes yesterday's news. But the propaganda monster is still there. The blueprint is a highly successful template—and extremely dangerous. And you can be sure that at this very moment, somewhere in the world, people are thinking about how they can refine and optimize the blueprint, thanks to ever-new digital possibilities. As long as the electorate can be—and is—manipulated in such a perfidious and planned way, there will be no peaceful moment for liberal democracies and open societies. All these findings are far-reaching.

This is where we usually get to the positives. The soothing balm after the shock. The motivational happy ending. Wiser thinkers have already formulated such final chapters—democracy needs to be strengthened, government needs to be de-bureaucratized, more participation and referendums, more resistance, political education, and so on.

But in light of the propaganda blueprint presented, we must doubt whether these catchphrases are potent enough as an antidote. Moreover, the approach would have to be as conceptually comprehensive as the propaganda it seeks to combat, and that would require a book of its own, at the very least. Moreover, it is debatable whether such an approach should be made public—because the propagandists don't do that either. The formula—or the prescriptions—for dealing with this in society remains unwritten in this book. It is, therefore, all the clearer that there is an urgent need for an intensive political, academic, and media debate.

For the reader, however, *Propaganda Decoded*— hopefully—provides a tool kit that sharpens the individual's perception and personal awareness of propaganda, its hidden goals, the interrelationships of various elements, and its patterns. When dealing with political communication, one should always be aware: Human beings are highly susceptible to psychological influence—whether en masse or as individuals. They are susceptible for social and group-dynamic reasons because they are motivated to perceive themselves as "right" or even superior. That is how the brain works—as demonstrated by cognitive biases, e. g., the confirmation bias and the illusory truth effect. Social media has created mechanisms that deliberately and mercilessly exploit psychological processes. Their algorithms are optimized to maximize views and dwell times, reaching for advertising with the aim of profit.

For democracy, this is an exposed flank that propagandists are abusing. They play with people's perceptions and psychological makeup for the pure purpose of manipulation and unquestioning allegiance.

So it is on all these human weaknesses and newer technical possibilities that the immense arsenal of weapons of the propaganda parties is directed: starting with the political idea that places the party outside the spectrum with the secret aim of gaining power for power's sake. Added to this is the use of conspiracy allegations raised in the same way against the top and the outside. They serve as meta-frames, oversize interpretive frames into which individual events are interpreted daily to serve as supposed evidence. The breaking of communication norms, such as the norm of fact-oriented communication or the norm of metacommunicative integration, which views political debates from a bird's-eye view, is particularly effective because successful political debates are essential for social dialogue and liberal democracies. This superstructure leads to a confusion of lies and truth. In this confusion, propagandists lie constantly, but also—to maximize the effect—tell the truth at unexpected moments so most people become tired and only perceive politics emotionally. Once they stop checking and start believing, they quickly fall into the realm of propaganda parties and become putty in their hands. Propaganda parties strive to make central lies accurate by piling facts about their actions on the fiction of the lie. Mirror reflexes or the paradoxical interplay of a chain of authentication and plausible deniability have been mentioned here as methods that give propaganda politicians maximum credibility with minimum accountability. All these are how propaganda wages war against the open society of liberal democracies, including norm-makers, fact-gatherers, and world-interpreters. Social media has replaced the mass meetings of earlier times. Propaganda politicians and their entourage abuse social media as a space of mass psychological contagion. They deliberately stir up, trigger, and serve disinhibited mass behavior by constantly filling their meta-frames to generate followers. To this end, they use quandaries against independent media. They also employ diffusion chambers, spillover tactics, and staircase argumentation.

The propaganda master plan is a political reality. It is used to charge and incite tens of millions of people daily—today, right now—against the open society of liberal democracies. This manipulative master plan has spread like wildfire across Western countries over the past quarter century, though not only there. The methodological references to Nazi Germany's propaganda are as verifiable as they are alarming. The propaganda machines cast a dark shadow over liberal democracies. The unrestrained excesses of Russia's war propaganda, which must be called totalitarian, should not obscure the fact that liberal democracies of the Western model have been and are being put under enormous pressure by similar means—primarily by forces at home. There is no reason to assume propaganda will go away or stay away. It is too compelling, successful, and seductive, especially for politicians and parties who seek power for power's sake and know no scruples. The danger is here. Always. Anyone who wants to stand for democracy, defend it, and work for a successful social dialogue outside propagandized friend-foe schemes must understand the propaganda of the present in its complexity and subtleties. May this book contribute to understanding and fighting this many-headed and many-armed monster.

Sources and Notes

Introduction

1 Check:
   - Steven Levitsky and Daniel Ziblatt, *How Democracies Die* (Crown, 2018)
   - Anne Applebaum, *Twilight of Democracy: The Seductive Lure of Authoritarianism* (Doubleday, 2020)
   - Yascha Mounk, *The People vs. Democracy* (Harvard University Press, 2018)
2 Giovanni Di Lorenzo "Es wird schwieriger." *Die Zeit*, 12.4.2022, 1.
3 Aro, *Putin's Trolls*, 14.
4 Sösemann, *Propaganda*, Vol. 2, 754.

Chapter 1

1 Aro, *Putin's Trolls*, 194 ff.
2 James Titcomb, "Governments in 30 Countries Are Paying 'Keyboard Armies' to Spread Propaganda, Report Says," *The Telegraph*, November 14, 2017.
3 Applebaum, *Twilight of Democracy*, Chapter III.; Pomerantsev, *This Is Not Propaganda*, 194 f.
4 Arendt, *Origins of Totalitarianism*, Part Three, Chapter Eleven.

Chapter 2

1 Kracauer, *Totalitäre Propaganda*, 34
2 Kracauer, *Totalitäre Propaganda*, 34
3 Arendt, *Origins of Totalitarianism*, 251

4 Arendt, *Origins of Totalitarianism*, 357

5 Hitler, *Struggle*, Vol. 2 Ch. 11

6 Kracauer, *Totalitäre Propaganda*, 39

7 Kracauer, *Totalitäre Propaganda*, 37

8 Sösemann, *Propaganda*, L I I

9 quoted in: Kracauer, *Totalitäre Propaganda*, 32. Very similar to Trump's: "Wasn't anybody an American anymore?" (Wolff, *Fire and Fury*, 62)

10 quoted in: Kracauer, *Totalitäre Propaganda*, 33

11 Thumann, *Der neue Nationalismus*, 214

12 Thumann, *Der neue Nationalismus*, 215

13 Vetter, *Nationalismus im Osten*, 79 ff.

14 Bax, *Volksverführer*, 216–218

15 Wolff, *Fire and Fury*, 310

16 quoted in: Johnston, *It's Even Worse Than You Think*, 261

17 http://www.talk-republik.de/Rechtspopulismus/docs/03/AfD-Strategie-2017.pdf, 3–5

18 https://www.focus.de/politik/deutschland/neuer-strategie-beschluss-20-prozent-afd-spitze-gibt-ambitioniertes-wahlziel-aus-und-will-sich-der-spd-annaehern_id_11060065.html & https://www.tagesspiegel.de/politik/internesstrategie papier-warum-die-afd-vom-marsch-durch-dieorgani sationen-traeumt/25246594.html

19 https://www.welt.de/politik/deutschland/article239911805/Baden-Wuerttemberg-Verfassungsschutz-stuft-AfD-als Verdachtsobjekt-ein.html

20 https://www.bpb.de/politik/grundfragen/parteien-indeutschland/afd/273131/wahlergebnisse-und-waehlerschaft

Chapter 3

1 Levitsky and Ziblatt, *How Democracies Die*, Chapter 7

2 Levitsky and Ziblatt, *How Democracies Die*, 45

3 Ulrich Steinkohl, Jörg Blank, and Basil Wegener, *Laschet: Planungsbeschleunigung wird Schwerpunkt in*

ersten 100 Tagen. German Press Agency dpa, August 21, 2021

4 Party Manifesto: *Alternative für Deutschland Bundesvorstand (2016): AfD-Manifest 2017. Die Strategie der AfD für das Wahljahr 2017.* http://www.talk-republik.de/Rechts populismus/docs/03/AfD-Strategie-2017.pdf

5 quoted in: Thumann, *Der neue Nationalismus*, 261

6 quoted in: Johnston, *It's Even Worse Than You Think*, 250

7 Adam Hodges, *When Words Trump Politics. Resisting a Hostile Regime of Language.* (Stanford: Stanford University Press, 2020)

8 Hodges, *When Words*, 33

Chapter 4

1 See Benz (*Protokolle*) and also Evans (*Hitler Conspiracies*) for more conspiracy allegations espoused by the nazi state.

2 Lamberty and Nocun, *Fake Facts*, 29 ff. & Butter, *Conspiracy Theories*, Chapter 4

3 Butter, *Conspiracy Theories*, Chapter 4

4 Butter, *Conspiracy Theories*, Chapter 4

5 Lamberty and Nocun, *Fake Facts*, 24

6 Morris, *The Return.* See: Sections XI–XV, Pages 173–186

7 see also: Butter, *Conspiracy Theories*, Chapter 2

8 Butter, *Conspiracy Theories*, Chapter 1

9 https://www.boell.de/de/2020/11/09/autoritaere-dynamiken-alte-ressentiments-neue-radikalitaet

Chapter 5

1 See for critical asessments: Arendt, *Origins of Totalitarianism*, and Kracauer, *Totalitäre Propaganda*

2 quoted in: Kracauer, *Totalitäre Propaganda*, 61

3 quoted in: Longerich, *Goebbels* 617

4 Kracauer, *Totalitäre Propaganda*, 59 f.

5 Goebbels, Joseph, *Der Angriff. Aufsätze aus der Kamp-*

fzeit (Munich: Zentralverlag der NSDAP, 1935),
322–324

6 Butter, *Conspiracy Theories*, Chapter 1
7 https://www.zeit.de/politik/ausland/2021-12/russland-
ukraine-grenze-militaeruebung-wintermanoever; https://
www1.wdr.de/nachrichten/ukraine-konflikt108.html
8 https://www.washingtonpost.com/politics/how-fact
checker-tracked-trump-claims/2021/01/23/ad04b69a5c1d-
11eb-a976-bad6431e03e2_story.html
9 quoted in: Hodges, *When Words Trump Politics*, 5
10 Hodges, *When Words Trump Politics*, 61
11 https://www.faz.net/aktuell/politik/inland/merkel-
meinungsfreiheit-heisst-nicht-widerspruchsverbot-
16469978.html
12 Applebaum, *Twilight of Democracy*, 7
13 ditto, 44 ff.
14 Nocun and Lamberty, *Fake Facts*, 72
15 Fazio et al., 993–1002
16 Fazio/Sherry, 1150–1160
17 quoted in: Kracauer, *Totalitäre Propaganda*, 61
18 Arendt, *Origins of Totalitarianism*, 333
19 Kracauer, *Totalitäre Propaganda*, 62

Chapter 6

1 Applebaum, *Twilight of Democracy*, Chapter II
2 https://www.derstandard.at/story/2000096296901/wie-
george-soros-viktororbans-feindbild-wurde
3 https://www.wiwo.de/politik/europa/us-milliardaer-
orbn-gegen-soros/20490804-4.html
4 https://www.derstandard.at/story/2000096296901/wie-
george-soros-viktororbans-feindbild-wurde
5 https://www.nzz.ch/international/die-eu-und-der-
angebliche-soros-plan-ld.1320976
6 Arendt, *Origins of Totalitarianism*, Part Three, Chapter
Eleven
7 Arendt, *Elemente und Ursprünge*, 948 (footnote in revised
German edition, not present in U.S. edition)

Chapter 7

1 Goebbels (1934), 178
2 Goebbels (1939), "Großmacht Presse", 2.9.1929, 197
3 Mounk, *The People vs. Democracy*, 67
4 Mounk, *The People vs. Democracy*, 69
5 Goebbels (1939), 73
6 ditto, 73
7 ditto, 71
8 https://www.news.com.au/world/north-america/us-
   politics/donald-trump-addresses-rioters-calls-them-very-
   special/news-story/74de85d24a4c143f2a58e9a3e3b72f01?
   fbclid=IwAR19J3NvSMulhuHhCzAHKLbvXrE1NzNoz
   vvDwpmBFU4jztxvEcyvYLbx9VI
9 Aro, *Putin's Trolls*, Chapter 14
10 Wolff, *Fire and Fury*, 62
11 Arendt, *Elemente und Ursprünge*, 826

Chapter 8

1 https://de.statista.com/infografik/19568/tweets-pro-
   jahrund-tag-von-donald-trump/
2 https://www.fr.de/politik/donald-trump-twitter-geschichte
   eines-social-media-meisters-13338088.html
3 Hillje, 94
4 https://www.dw.com/de/afd-die-macht-in-den-sozialen-
   medien/a-58906678
5 Bax, 95
6 Le Bon, *The Crowd*, 29
7 Le Bon, *The Crowd*, 34
8 Oddo, *The Discourse of Propaganda*
9 Le Bon, *The Crowd*, 36
10 Le Bon, *The Crowd*, 40
11 Le Bon, *The Crowd*, 60
12 Canetti, *Crowds and Power*, 49 ff.
13 Brudermann, 4
14 Aro, *Putin's Trolls* 22
15 Pomerantsev, *This is Not Propaganda*, 125 f.

16 Frenkel, Kang, *Ugly Truth* 337
17 Frenkel, Kang, *Ugly Truth*, 219
18 Le Bon, *The Crowd*, 82
19 https://www.deutschlandfunk.de/trump-und-die-republikaner-mehr-eine-sekte-als-eine-partei-100.html; https://www.t-online.de/nachrichten/ausland/usa/id_89400100/us-republikaner-im-kriegszustand-donaldtrumps-saat-zerreisst-die-republikaner.html
20 Le Bon, *The Crowd*, 128
21 Le Bon, *The Crowd*, 72
22 Le Bon, *The Crowd*, 45
23 Le Bon, *The Crowd*, Book II, Chapter I

Chapter 9

1 quoted in: Bax, 167
2 https://www.spiegel.de/politik/ausland/wladimir-putin-ueber-homosexualitaet-wirklich-absolut-unvoreingenommen-a-1275022.html
3 Arendt, *Origins of Totalitarianism*, 326
4 Arendt, *Origins of Totalitarianism*, 311 (footnotes)
5 https://www.spiegel.de/ausland/wahlkampf-in-den-usa-donald-trump-nennt-biden-einen-staatsfeind-a-a81e35616f61-417d-ae02-7d88b948a81f

Literature

Some dates in the references are misleading because they are reprints of classics that appeared much earlier. Arendt's *Elements and Origins of Total Domination* was originally published in 1951, Canetti's *Mass and Power* in 1960, Kracauer wrote *Totalitarian Propaganda* between 1936 and the winter of 1937, and Le Bon published *Psychology of the Crowd* in 1895.

Akyol, Çiğdem. *Erdoğan. Die kritische Biografie.* Freiburg (Germany): Herder, 2018

Alternative für Deutschland Bundesvorstand. *AfD – Manifest 2017. Die Strategie der AfD für das Wahljahr 2017.* http://www.talk-republik.de/Rechtspopulismus/ docs/03/AfD-Strategie-2017.pdf

Applebaum, Anne. *Twilight of Democracy, The Seductive Lure of Authoritarianism.* New York: Anchor, 2021

Arendt, Hannah. *The Origins Of Totalitarianism.* New York: Meridian Books, The World Publishing Company, 1962 https://cheirif.files.wordpress.com/2014/08/hannah-arendt-the-origins-of-totalitarianism-meridian-1962.pdf

Arendt, Hannah. *Elemente und Ursprünge totaler Herrschaft.* Fankfurt a.M. (Germany): Europäische Verlagsanstalt, 2009 https://www.scribd.com/document/382741667/ARENDT-Hannah-Elemente-Und-Ursprunge-Totaler-Herrschaft-2011

Aro, Jessikka. *Putin's Trolls: On the Frontlines of Russia's Information War Against the World.* New York: Ig Publishing, 2022

Bax, Daniel. *Die Volksverführer. Warum Rechtspopulisten so erfolgreich sind.* Frankfurt (Germany): Westend, 2018

Benz, Wolfgang. *Die Protokolle der Weisen von Zion. Die Legende von der jüdischen Weltverschwörung.* Munich (Germany): C. H. Beck, 2007

Butter, Michael. *The Nature of Conspiracy Theories;* New York: Polity, 2020

Brudermann, Thomas. *Massenpsychologie. Psychologische Ansteckung, kollektive Dynamiken, Simulationsmodelle.* Wien, Austria: Springer, 2010

Canetti, Elias. *Crowds and Power.* New York: Farrar, Strauss and Giroux, 1984

De Weck, Roger. *Die Kraft der Demokratie. Eine Antwort auf die autoritären Reaktionäre.* Berlin (Germany): Suhrkamp, 2020

Evans, Richard J. *The Hitler Conspiracies.* Oxford, UK: Oxford University Press, 2020

Fazio, Lisa K. et al. "Knowledge Does Not Protect Against Illusory Truth." *Journal of Experimental Psychology General* Vol. 144 (2015), No. 5, 993–1002

Fazio, Lisa K., Sherry, Carrie L. "The Effect of Repetition on Truth Judgments Across Development" *Psychological Science* 31, No. 9 (September 2020): 1150–1160

Frenkel, Sheera, and Cecilia Kang. *An Ugly Truth: Inside Facebook's Battle for Domination.* New York: Harper 2021

Goebbels, Joseph. *Kampf um Berlin: der Anfang.* Munich (Germany): Franz Eher, 1934

Goebbels, Joseph. *Der Angriff. Aufsätze aus der Kampfzeit.* Munich (Germany): Franz Eher, 1939

Hillje, Johannes. *Propaganda 4.0. Wie rechte Populisten Politik machen.* Bonn (Germany): Dietz, 2018

Hitler, Adolf. My Struggle. (Translated into English by James Murphy, 1939) https://gutenberg.net.au/ebooks02/0200601h.html#ch2-11

Hodges, Adam. *When Words Trump Politics. Resisting a Hostile Regime of Language.* Stanford: Stanford University Press, 2020

Johnston, David Cay. *It's Even Worse Than You Think: What the Trump Administration is Doing to America.* New York: Simon and Schuster, 2018

Kracauer, Siegfried. *Totalitäre Propaganda*. Berlin (Germany): Suhr-Kamp, 2013

Le Bon, Gustave. *The Crowd*. London: T. F. Unwin,ltd, 1926[1]

Levitsky, Steven, and Daniel Ziblatt. *How Democracies Die*. New York: Crown Publishing Group, 2018

Longerich, Peter. *Goebbels, A Biography*. New York: Random House, 2015

Morris, Dick. *The Return. Trump's Big 2024 Comeback*. West Palm Beach: Humanix Books, 2022

Mounk, Yascha. *The People vs Democracy: Why Our Freedom is in Danger and How to Save it*. Cambridge: Harvard University Press, 2018

Müller, Jan-Werner. *What is Populism?* Philadelphia: University of Pennsylvania Press, 2016

Nocun, Katharina, and Pia Lamberty. Fake Facts. Wie Verschwörungstheorien unser Denken bestimmen. Cologne (Germany): Quadriga, 2020

Oddo, John. *The Discourse of Propaganda*. University Park, PA: PennState Press, 2018

Pomerantsev, Peter. *This Is Not Propaganda: Adventures in the War Against Reality*. New York: PublicAffairs, 2019

Sösemann, Bernd. *Propaganda – Medien und Öffentlichkeit in der NS-Diktatur. Mitarbeit: Marius Lange. Beiträge zur Kommunikationsgeschichte, Band 25.* Stuttgart (Germany): Franz Steiner Verlag, 2011

Thumann, Michael. *Der neue Nationalismus. Die Wiederkehr einer totgeglaubten Ideologie*. Berlin (Germany): Die Andere Bibliothek, 2020

Vetter, Reinhold. *Nationalismus im Osten Europas. Was Kaczyński und Orbán mit Le Pen und Wilders verbindet*. Berlin (Germany): Ch. Links, 2017

Wolff, Michael. *Fire and Fury. Inside the Trump White House*. London: Little, Brown, 2018

Woodward, Bob and Robert Acosta. *Peril*. New York: Simon & Schuster, 2021

Author Birand Bingül received a degree in journalism with a minor in American Studies at the University of Dortmund. As a reporter, he has worked for the German station Tagesschau and also served as deputy corporate spokesman of the network WDR and as head of communications of the network ARD. He is currently managing director of the media company fischerAppelt, advisors. Bingül is the author of several books.

Translator Oliver Latsch spent the first six years of his life in Zambia and Kenya, before moving to Hamburg, Germany. He studied ecology and conservation at the University of Sussex and completed a PhD in ecology at Imperial College in London. He lives with his family in Los Angeles, California.